Manila, Goodbye

Manila, Goodbye

Robin Prising

Illustrated with Photographs

HOUGHTON MIFFLIN COMPANY BOSTON

1975

Library of Congress Cataloging in Publication Data

Prising, Robin.   Manila, goodbye.

1. Philippine Islands—History—Japanese occupation,
1942–1945—Personal narratives. 2. Prising, Robin.
I. Title.
DS686.4.P74   915.99'03'350924 [B]   74–28236
ISBN 0-395-20432-1

Printed in the United States of America

W 10 9 8 7 6 5 4 3 2 1

This book is for

WILLIAM LEO COAKLEY

and dedicated to the memory of

FREDERIC WILLIAM PRISING

1878–1954

and

MARIE LESLIE PRISING

1883–1963

as well as to
the unknown parents
who gave me
life

Contents

Illustrations follow page 182

Manila, Goodbye

Prologue

"All things fall and are built again."

—WILLIAM BUTLER YEATS

1945, MANILA BAY . . . On this April day the skies are dead; there is no wind or weather. The piers have been bombed out and this great harbor is a devastation of sunken ships; prows, masts, funnels and sterns jut out from the bay. Yet the minesweepers have done their work; they have made safe a lane for us that leads to the open sea. We stand silent and huddled together in this landing-craft that speeds past the shipwrecks, taking us out to a transport that is bound for the United States. I stare back towards land, watching Manila recede from me — iron skeletons of buildings, gutted churches, smashed homes. Out of the wreckage an occasional house stands whole, spared from the ravages of war, scarcely singed by the fire.

Here I am, a twelve-year-old boy wearing a man's military boots — they are too big for my feet. This army surplus uniform is absurdly big for me. Only the cap fits. Beneath this precocious brat, who is so eager for life and too willing to play the braggart with his experiences, is a person half in hiding, a spoilt child who was taken prisoner of war and has become a refugee. He has seen death; he has known fear; he has had enough of hunger. Within him welters a confusion of wonder and bitterness which the brat could not brag about if he tried.

To the left, in the far distance, beyond the ruins, I see the cross on the tower of Santo Tomás — our prison camp. Throughout my life it shall remain with me, directly before the mind's eye, a symbol and a lesson. The worst is over now. I keep gazing back through parched, stinging eyes, with a mouthful of salt big enough to choke me. I do not want to bury the dead; I refuse to allow them to be turned into a memory. Let them stink there forever; let the world go sick from their stench. Why — ? Because this must not ever happen again.

In the desolate city which I have outlived, which I am leaving behind, people are staggering over the stones in the rubble, burying the bones, picking up the rags of their lives, scouring for salvage, determined to begin again. Already they have begun to build. They are constructing sheds and hovels, temporary shelters, making use of tin cans, charred beams, scraps of corrugated iron; they are building from the waste laid by the American and Japanese armies.

Only the dead cannot start again. Their corpses lie buried in the field at Santo Tomás; they are trapped in the broken buildings and piled under rubbish heaps in the streets. You can still smell them in some quarters of the city, rotting in the tropic heat. The dead are the losers; it is they who have lost the war. They are all victims — Filipinos, American and Japanese alike. And the dead shall be forgotten: their faces shall be forgotten, their names, their deeds of hatred or of love. They defy statistics; their number may only be estimated. For us, the winners, the survivors, the dead have become wounds in our memories, wounds that time shall close and heal. And time shall turn them into the scars of memory or the words in a book. This knowledge fills me with nausea: the yeasty smell of baking bread after months of starvation was not so sickening.

Manila fades before me. Now from the deck of the departing troopship *Mormacsea* I hang at the rail staring back. The graveyard city, which was once my home, shrinks to a grey outline and, although I still can distinguish the shapes of its battered buildings, they have become a remote silhouette. When I think of the dead, those everlasting sleepers, a ruthless pride jumps in my veins — the ridiculous pride of personal survival, the pride of being alive. Everyone who lives is lucky.

Over thirty years have passed . . . Under the same sun, on the banks of the same river, another Manila thrives in place of the one I left behind. Steep white buildings rise where the rubble lay and some of the mangled bridges, the ancient gateways and churches have been rebuilt, copied or refaced. In the past third of a century a new generation has grown to manhood. Manila, the most devastated city in Asia, has risen from the ashes; its population has doubled. The dead are replaced twice over.

But children do not forget: the voice of the child speaks through the man I have become. I cannot resurrect the dead or the lost city, nor can I write their history, though perhaps in the chronicle of my childhood some part of them may live again. The child cries out, and when I hear his shouts he reminds me that the pleasures we shared were quite as rich as the pains, as natural, as inexorable, as the days and nights through which we, the living, pass.

Manila — *Mabuhay!* Childhood city. I hurrah you in your Tagalog tongue. *Mabuhay:* long may you live! Again I hear the heft of your bells, those frantic bells from Spanish churches; I hear them with the ringing pain of the past. They ring from the north and south of the Pasig River. They strike the hour and the Angelus, they toll the citizenry of Manila to mass.

At dawn, rousing the city like a bugler, comes the call of the crowing cock — I can hear all Manila waking. While the breadman cries his wares through the streets, *"Pan de Sal,"* the clatter of wooden shoes echoes from the pavement — Filipinos off to early mass. In the mornings of my days I listen to the bastinado of horses' hoofs, the crack of the coachman's whip, the creaky wheels of horse carriages — the *carromatas, calesas* and *carretelas* as they come jogging by.

On the stroke of two, the siesta is over and however fiercely the sun beats down on trams, courtyards and thoroughfares, the shops in the city unshutter. There is no respite from the heat until the huge ball of fire burns its way slowly west and sets in splendor behind Mariveles Mountain, the Bataan peninsula and Corregidor. Then the cool breeze comes, gulls scavenge the shore and over the city in each tall belfry leap randy gangs of bells, driving battalions of bats from their bell towers, from their caves in far suburbs, shaking a panic of blind, wobbling flight overhead. In the districts of Manila — Intramuros, Quiapo, Santa Cruz, Malaté, Tondo, Ermita, Binondo — women cover their heads with their hands and run home, frightened lest a bat web itself into their hair.

To the west, in the bay, lights from the ships at anchor stipple the waves; night sheds its darkness over Manila, a city built on the ruins of a lost Mohammedan settlement, the proud seaport of South-East Asia, called by her lovers the Pearl in the Orient Seas.

As It Was in the Beginning

A Privileged Childhood

1.

MY BIRTH IS A SECRET. On Sunday, the twelfth of March 1933, at St. Paul's Hospital in Vancouver, Canada, the cord of a newborn boy was cut from its mother and tied. Shortly after the infant was born, its stomach shut with a spasm and had to be opened by a surgeon's knife. The child survived. It waited for six months, unwanted, and then was taken for adoption.

News of the world on the day I was born heralded the catastrophes of the future. On that Sunday in Berlin Hitler first flew the swastika flag over the Reichstag: the Nazis had won the German elections. In London a crowd jeered the Japanese envoy, Matsuoka: Japan was pressing its plan to quit the League of Nations. On the high seas, somewhere between Japan and America, the ships of the United States Navy were ready for the greatest war maneuvers in the history of the Pacific.

What were the circumstances of my birth? They were not mentioned in the Sunday papers. If the names of my original parents are known, they are sealed in the secret files of the Bureau of Vital Statistics. I detest secrets. For years I have imagined every possibility about my origins, from romantic love to sordid rape, only to conclude that, whatever the case, the truth is neither pure nor simple.

AM BRINGING HOME BONNIE BANTLING BOY
ARRIVING TUESDAY IN EMPRESS OF JAPAN

With this cable, Frederic William Prising was presumably informed that his wife was returning to Manila with an adopted son. But what had my adoptive mother been doing in Vancouver at all? Mother travelled for pleasure and Vancouver is a port for ships bound to the Far East.

The only time I questioned my father about the adoption he sent me to ask my mother. She was talkative, elusive and contradictory. Although she gave the impression of a dainty princess, Mother had been on the stage before the first Great War; she had played in Shakespeare and costume dramas. She loved legends and ignored facts and, besides, her own origins were obscure. She told me white lies or half-truths, hinting that I was "sired by a youth with some strain of Jew or Gipsy in him" whom, at various times, she placed as an itinerant student, merchant mariner, circus barker or forester. Of one thing she seemed certain: I was born of a girl aged seventeen, wicked and unwed, but from a good Catholic family. Then, sweeping the subject aside with a sneer at heredity, she would deliver odes on the virtues of my environment. I am convinced that Mother knew the truth. And yet I did not suspect that she would take the secret down to the grave with her. Somewhere among her wills and codicils, her moonstones and osprey crests, I expected to discover a formal message with the story of my birth, penned in her Victorian, slanting hand.

The band was playing at Manila's old Pier Seven when my mother and I arrived aboard the Canadian Pacific liner, the *Empress of Japan,* an imperious white ship, the largest and fastest on the Pacific. Father was at the pier to meet us, with a doctor to vaccinate me and two nurses, nuns, to tend me for the first few days. I, of course, remember nothing of this, but our arrival was reported in the press and, before long, rumors circulated among Mother's friends. She had told each a slightly different story, the broad outlines of which were the same, although the finer points were shaded to suit the characters of the persons told.

My first impressions seem to go back to a hospital in Manila: white-robed nuns floating out of whiter walls, the plaster and gauze over the vaccination on my right leg. But memory begins with Napoleon, a proud paragon of a cockatoo flying at me as I sit in my playpen — o jealous white bird with saffron crest. The cockatoo is chained to his perch and cannot reach me. I know he has lived in this house long before I came into it and that he is impatient for my papa to come home and feed him black and yellow seeds. Fascinated and unafraid, the baby in his pen is watching the cockatoo, dimly aware that we are both prisoners.

Long before I knew the meanings of words, my mother would linger at my bedside holding a book in her hands, reciting nursery rhymes. She rarely troubled to glance down at a page for she knew rhymes, poems and whole tales by heart. With her light, warm English voice she woke my love for the mood and music of words, she nurtured the earliest shoots and tendrils of my imagination. She could pronounce the syllables of the language perfectly and spontaneously, and by nimbly changing pace, with a glide here, the merest trace of a pause, or a delicately shaded inflection, she made words come alive. I do not remember when first I learned the songs from Shakespeare's plays, for my mother's voice had lilted into the merry notes of "Under the Greenwood Tree" and echoed through the grave cadences of the dirge from *Cymbeline* before I could tell the days of the week or the months of the year.

2.

Being an only child, I was extremely spoilt and happy, and apart from the bite of the tropical mosquito, the daily spoonful of Canadian cod-liver oil and an occasional dose of English physic, my memories up to the age of three are singularly pleasant. My father told me that when he was about to give up any hope of my ever saying "Pup-pa" or "Mum-ma," I astonished him by coming out with long sentences and batteries of questions. From then on, I never stopped talking.

When I was three years old, I experienced my first deep disappointment, one for which I would not forgive my parents, and it wakened my sympathy for the underdog. Into our home came a mongrel pup of soft and furry fawn with ears like a collie's. I fell instantly in love with him. Holding the creature in my arms, I was photographed in the garden beside my sandbox and pails, with Papa leaning over to stroke its head. The very next day my puppy disappeared. It would grow vicious, I was told; it was a common cur and unsafe with children, fit only for a watchdog in the servants' quarters. I rebelled with a terrible tantrum, shrieking that in that case *I* wished to live in the servants' quarters. My puppy was not returned but I was still asking after him a year later.

Pushing myself higher and higher as I stood in my swing, I pondered an impossible question, which no one was able to answer to my satisfaction. How, I wondered, could I distinguish one person from another? Of course, some people had dark hair and others fair; some eyes were blue, others brown — but I knew that the answer was far more complicated than that. Whenever my father came home at sundown, and the houseboy had fetched him his whisky, Father would feed Napoleon and attack the mosquitoes with a Flit gun while I badgered him with questions: Why is gold more costly than silver? Why is a ship's screw at her stern? If we can go to Hong Kong, why can't we go to the moon? And then there was the question that baffled me most: Why do people speak in different languages?

If I wanted facts, I did not go to my mother, for with her no fact, no explanation, was ever told twice in exactly the same way. Instinctively I questioned my father when I opened the *Illus-*

trated London News and discovered sepia-brown pictures of Guernica bombed and grim faces in the Spanish trenches. Father explained that even here, in Manila, many Spanish families were divided between loyalty to the Republican government and support of Generalísimo Franco. I could not understand the difference between the two sides and wondered whether the Spaniards in Manila would fight each other in the streets. When Mother overheard my questions about the war in Spain, the *Illustrated London News* was put out of my four-year-old reach and sight.

"Curiosity," my mother purred, "killed the cat." I misunderstood this vexing adage, thinking that *I* was curiosity and might kill a cat. By the time I turned four, my curiosity did lead me into a deed almost as cruel. A German governess was engaged to occupy my afternoons with the Greek myths and to give me German lessons. We sat on the verandah while the wind played on the Chinese chimes hanging above us. Fräulein Winkel was an attractive redhead with a screech of a voice. Since she was also a strict and determined young woman, we reached an impasse before the first week was out. "Today," Fräulein announced, "ve vill begin vit Pandora's box." I grew madly excited by the tale of the inquisitive Pandora opening up the forbidden box and releasing all the evils of the world. After Fräulein had finished I refused to let her go on to our German, but demanded a precise description of all these evils. "No! No! No!" she shrilled, and when I continued pestering her she picked up a fly swatter and snapped at me, "If you interrupt vonce more, I vill hit you vit zis!" Her Prussian ultimatum summoned up my blood. "Hit me with that," I retorted, "and I shall stick you with this badge." The Fräulein's amber eyes narrowed in anger and she struck me with the swatter, so I stuck her with my badge.

Squeals, German and piercing, brought Mother to the veran-

dah: she smacked me on the bottom, hastened me out of Fräulein Winkel's earshot and flared, "You'll rue this day, you
Bastard brat."

It was the first time I heard that word.

3.

Our life in prewar Manila was complacent and comfortable,
a life of pearl egg-spoons, sterling silver and servants. Today, it
seems a trifle foolish and eccentric, like some quaint and curious
period piece found in an attic. Mine was a child's world, cared
for and protected in every way. Money was never a problem —
except at table, where the subject was forbidden. The pennies I
was given for chocolates I placed in the palms of beggars on the
steps of baroque cathedrals, beggars covered with open sores and
sucking flies. They needed my pennies and I was afraid of their
sores. I pitied those beggars, just as I pitied the little match-girl
in the story, who dies of the cold.

At home there were only three of us — Father, Mother and
myself. Our homes were always alike, though we moved every
year or two, from apartments in an old Spanish house at Calle
Romero Salas, to a yellow villa with a view of Dewey Boulevard
and the ships in the bay and, shortly before the war, to a bungalow by the sea. Wherever we lived there was a wide verandah,
a spacious sitting room and dining room, three large bedrooms,
a nursery, a library and the servants' quarters. Every home smelt
of tea — Lapsang Souchong, Darjeeling and my mother's favorite, First Picking Flower tea. From the ceilings white electric
fans, like aeroplane propellers, kept the fragrant current of air
moving through the house, taking the curse off the tropic heat.
A Coromandel screen stood in one corner of the sitting room and
close to it, on a table, was the statue of Kwannon, goddess of
mercy, carved in white jade.

Punctual and plain, our meals were invariably Occidental:
crême soup, veal roast, carrots and blancmange. Mother did not

cook them; she ordered them every morning from our head boy, Alfredo. He it was who answered the telephone, did the marketing and cooking, waited at table and acted as butler when formality was required. At his recommendation a succession of houseboys was hired and fired. They aired the sheets, made the beds, swept and dusted; they pared the vegetables and did the washing up. But Alfredo kept the brass and silver gleaming (he trusted no one with this task) and twice a month he skated over the floors with coconut husks strapped to his bare feet. Whenever I gazed in envy, Alfredo broke into a golden-toothed grin, for he knew that I was strictly forbidden this perilous game.

During my first eight years, there was never a boy next door. My companions were always grown-up: amahs, yayas or governesses. Until I was three, we had Ah-Yee, my Chinese amah. She gave me my bottle (Bear Brand milk from Switzerland), changed me when I was wet and bathed me, sparing my mother such dreary duties. Ah-Yee took me out on bright days and once stood me up in my wicker pram for a snapshot — among the few mementos of those days to survive the war. Ah-Yee was briefly replaced by another nursemaid, who was found wanting in imagination and left our employ for a position with a military family. Then came Terray (her name rhymes with "sigh") , my Filipina yaya. No trace of Terray remains except for my vivid memories of her: the round Visayan face, gold-hooped earrings and starched white dress. She was my companion, my earliest friend. Together we explored sad cemeteries and the interiors of Spanish churches, and I taught her every new word I had learned. At the age of five I cried, "Individuality, Terray. Individuality!" But she could not pronounce it. "In duality," she would say.

Terray and I had our secrets, the *binabay* in particular, whom we encountered on one of our walking tours through the streets of Manila. The binabay were a bevy of painted and gilded young men; they slithered and giggled, reeked of cheap scent and apparently took nothing seriously.

"Who are they, Terray?"

"Very bad boys — they steal the husband from the wife."

"Would they try to steal Daddy from Mummy?"

"Do not tell to your mother," Terray said quickly. "Your Mama, she don't know anything about bad-class people."

Terray, of course, was wrong. Though Mother forbade her to let me play with ill-mannered children, my mother was scarcely so innocent as she appeared. And I was very young when I first gave her away. For once, when Mother opened a morning kindergarten at our home, I called another boy "bastard brat" in a tantrum.

"Where did you learn such language?" asked the mistress my mother engaged for this select group of English and Canadian children.

"From my mother," I replied.

She was a remarkable woman, my mother. Intuitive and warm, she was an elusive creature of sudden moods, swift to anger and swift to sympathy. She was also used to getting her own way. Her nature was as unpredictable as the English weather and as varied as her English countryside, where within short distances of each other lie downs, flatlands, wolds, heaths and the seaside. Part bitch, part angel. Most people, including my father, saw only the angel. And yet if she gave the impression of being a nice woman, thank God she was not!

One scarcely expected anyone who remembered Queen Victoria's Diamond Jubilee, and had seen the fat old lady in black riding in her carriage out of Buckingham Palace, to have a clinically modern candor about sex. In the convent at Wantage where she was educated, the girls were not permitted to take their baths in the nude but were obliged to soap themselves beneath linen smocks. Against this early training, however, my mother had rebelled: as a young child I was frequently allowed to run about the house and garden stark naked. Once, when I was three, she took me into her saltwater bath aboard ship. This experiment was not repeated after I frightened her from the tub by diving for her black spot and demanding a lesson in the geography of the body. Years later she told me how she had been introduced to the perils of sex by her mother who was a sister (what is called a head nurse in America) at the Gower Street Hospital in London. As a girl fresh from her Wantage convent, my mother was taken on a tour of the venereal ward. Of her father she never spoke except once, when pressed. Then she made vague allusions to his being killed in a gasworks when she was an infant. Not until after her own death did I discover the dark Victorian secret she had kept for nearly eighty years: like me, she was illegitimate.

No one knew that Mother was in her fiftieth year when she brought me to Manila, for until the war she looked considerably younger. In her youth, at the opening of the century, she had posed for artists and illustrators, even for those flowery post cards of the period — demure valentines of the rosemary-for-remembrance variety. Beneath her rich mass of dark hair, her blue eyes were deep set in natural shadows. They were amazing eyes, haunting, mysterious and expressive of her many moods. Wherever she went in those lost days in the Far East before the war, Mother was accorded that special deference reserved for the Lovely Lady.

4.

Motoring, as we still called it in the thirties, was among the chief pleasures of my childhood. If at first I accepted the Chrysler Imperial, as children accept familiar things, later I grew more houseproud, for I noticed that our black and tan limousine was rather larger than most cars we passed.

When I was four years old, Mother and I, with our chauffeur, Ambrosio, went up in the Chrysler to Baguio, summer capital of the Philippines, where everyone who was supposed to be anyone spent the hot season high among the pines and mountains. The last lap of the eight-hour drive from Manila twists up a narrow road of multiple treacherous turns called the Zig-Zag.

Hooting the Klaxon to warn of our massive approach, Ambrosio maneuvered the eight-cylinder Chrysler up the Zig-Zag with the zest of a flying ace. At every screech of the brakes, Mother would cry, "Ambrosio, dear boy — not so fast! Not so fast!" but I spurred him on, shouting, "Faster — oh, much faster, Ambrosio. We're not going nearly fast enough."

It began growing dusk as we arrived at Baguio. Smoke wreathed from the chimneys of summer villas, and the wizened mountain people, the Igorotes, were coming back from market in the dim light, winding their way up the trails to their mountain homes. Small as gnomes, they were barely visible in the settling dark and I could scarcely wait to see them by day.

Next morning, shafts of sunlight broke through the pines as I ran out to find the Igorotes already on their way to market, filing down the footpaths in their bright loincloths, carrying babies, blankets and caged mountain dogs. For me, the Igorotes were like real live Indians — and I was scared of them too, for some, I knew, were still head-hunters and Ambrosio had warned me that they would kidnap me if they got a chance.

"Igorotes *eat* those dogs — isn't it dreadful?" Mother said. "Why when first I came up here with Daddy, we actually saw them roasting the poor doggies. Dreadful!"

But what most impressed me at Baguio was not the Igorotes or the Benguet gold mines and not even the thousand-year-old rice terraces built into the hills by the Ifugao — it was Miss Adeline Mumby. Mother and I were sitting on the post office steps, licking stamps for letters, when Miss Mumby marched into our lives. Catching sight of this superb creature, Mother let fall her letters as if an electrical current had run through her. Miss Mumby was a tall, gawky woman clad in a necktie and shirt, herringbone tweeds and sturdy, well-scuffed walking shoes. Her wiry grey hair was worn in an Eton crop and she sported a Tyrolean hat with a jaunty feather. Miss Mumby wore, pinned to her jacket like a badge, a dusty cluster of artificial violets. She was not alone. Directly behind her stalked her constant companion, Victor, a huge police-dog. As Miss Mumby strode up the post office steps, Mother brightly rose and accosted her: "Aren't you English?"

Miss Mumby's monocle dropped from her left eye and with a jerky bow, as if clicking her heels, she paused and took us in with a doughty squint. "English? 'Course I am. From Leicester. This is my friend Victor." Her voice changed briskly, assuming the tone of a sergeant major. "Victor! Say how d'ye do to the lady and the small boy." Upon this command the dog promptly sat, proffered his paw, and barked. These introductions accomplished, I was dispatched to post Mother's and Miss Mumby's letters. When I returned, Miss Mumby and Victor were invited into our car and whisked off to the Pines Hotel for lunch.

Our appearance in the dining room caused a bit of a stir. Everyone stared. "They don't like Victor coming in here," Miss Mumby said, snorting, "so I told the management a thing or two and dared them to complain." Adeline Mumby surveyed the entire dining room through her monocle, then abruptly let it fall. "Never seen a dog in a dining room, have they?" I knew that if Victor made part of the sensation, Miss Mumby created the major share.

Adeline Mumby was the first woman I saw who chain-smoked (in those days it was still slightly outré for ladies to smoke in public at all). Her strong, square hands were as stained as her magnificently crooked teeth. Puffing away and crushing out the stumps, Miss Mumby told us that she had come out to the Orient "to get the feel of the atmosphere for my book. Crime shocker, you know. Murder takes place in the Yoshiwara — nice lot of shots and a stabbing. False clues lead to Manila first — it was most frightfully hot when we got there, so we came up here to cool off."

Although usually standoffish with strangers, Mother was remarkably keen on Miss Mumby — as indeed I was too. Mumby gave me curious vibrations; she was most distinguished and absolutely herself. Unlike other people, who were merely one thing or another, she was a splendid combination of the sexes. I kept remembering the swift sensation of attraction that ran through Mother like a shock. And yet, though they discovered that they had attended neighboring schools at Wantage a few years apart, they called each other only by their surnames and there was no suggestion of intimacy between them. Their relations remained slightly formal, sublimated by the conventions of lunch, tea and motoring and, alas, thoroughly circumspect.

In any case, one week at Baguio proved quite enough for Adeline Mumby. The Igorotes made her uneasy. "Beastly folk, those Igorotes — savages; only savages would eat dogs. They've got their eyes on my Victor. Pah! He'd gobble them up in a jiffy — they're such a *small* people."

A taxi drew up to the Pines Hotel. "Well, chin-chin! We're off to Singapore and I fancy I'll feel rather better there. It's Rangoon after that. My father got buried in some churchyard there, so I shall have to look him up. Ta-ta!" She was in the taxi now, Victor sitting beside her. "Keep in touch, mind," she called from the window. "Cheerio!" And with our farewells done, Miss Mumby and Victor were off in the taxi with her incredible assortment of luggage pasted with labels from Deauville to Kowloon.

5.

Father was a millionaire, according to legend, when he married Mother in 1912. Ever since the Spanish-American War, he had been amassing a fortune in the Philippines. As a lad of nineteen he left his native San Francisco with an uncle who persuaded him to try his luck in the Far East. There was an epidemic of cholera in Shanghai at the time they reached it; his uncle took ill and died. Convinced that China was cursed, Father fled Shanghai and cholera, shipping out to Manila in early 1898. Here the times worked in his favor: Manila was in a state of siege, the Filipinos were in rebellion against Spanish rule, and shortly thereafter Commodore Dewey sailed into Manila Bay and sank the Spanish fleet and the United States claimed the Philippine archipelago. Within a decade my father had made a good deal of money in tobacco and by importing horses from India; he held shares in the Jockey Club (of which he was a founding member) and became an advisor to the American governor general, William Howard Taft. In 1910 Father had come to New York on business — probably hunting a wife.

My parents met at the Criterion Theatre in February of 1911, when Mother was appearing with Constance Collier in *Thaïs*. She played three roles in the production — Phroë, a courtesan and friend to Thaïs, an Egyptian slave and a nun. No doubt Father was as intrigued by her versatility as by the fact that she was listed in the programme with three different stage names.

"That's the woman I shall marry," Father decided when Mother came on the stage. But it was not so easy. When he gave a party for the players at the Astor Hotel, she scarcely spoke to him but spent the evening reciting Shakespeare with Sydney Greenstreet, another English member of the company. A more intimate party followed, at the Brevoort, and this time Father managed to speak to her. Soon afterwards Mother found him waiting for her at the stage door in his civet greatcoat, a chauffeur at the wheel of his Panhard-Levassor.

From his photographs I should guess that Father was quite a dashing man about town — a trifle flash, perhaps, but certainly, as a rich tobacco man, a good catch for a young woman in the

precarious world of the stage. They married in June of the
following year and remained devoted to each other for the rest
of their lives. I can still hear their unmistakable voices as I
heard them in my childhood calling to each other, using their
quaint, spoony terms of endearment.

"Are you there, my true love?"

"Just here, beloved."

Leaving New York in 1914, my parents spent the spring in
Paris, Montreux and Venice on their way to Naples to embark
on the long sea voyage east of Suez. The day before they sailed,
an epoch had ended: the Archduke Franz Ferdinand, heir to the
Austrian throne, was shot at Sarajevo. My parents, however, believed that Europe was too civilized to go to war, that the
splendidly uniformed armies of the kaiser, the king and the czar
were merely there for show. Nor did the Great War that followed affect my parents' private lives, though their manners and
points of view soon grew out of date. Rich, elegant and slightly
démodé, they made their home in Manila for over forty years.

Restless by nature, Mother took to travelling again during
typhoon seasons and heat waves. Childless until my adoption,
she journeyed through China, across Russia via the Trans-
Siberian Railway, and over much of Europe. Though Father
accompanied her to India and on short trips to Siam and the
Malay States, her habitual travelling companions were Madame
Franck, the Belgian consul's wife, or Madame Yamaguchi, wife
of the Japanese consul at Harbin.

In the late twenties, when Father's business took a turn for
the worse, my parents' life of luxury came to an abrupt halt.
And yet, ever a lady of contradictions, Mother welcomed the
change. She had not enjoyed bridge parties and the social life
of the rich. Father's business reverses gave her the excuse to
teach drama and elocution — she pretended, however, that she
taught only for a hobby.

Her credentials for teaching were impeccable. At fifteen

mother had won a scholarship to Sir Frank Benson's Shakespearean Company at Stratford-upon-Avon and had spent the decade before her marriage on the stage. After her apprenticeship, Mother was recruited from the Bensonians to appear as the Player Queen in *Hamlet* with Forbes-Robertson on his first American tour. The greatest Hamlet of his time, Sir Johnston Forbes-Robertson was the only actor my mother really liked. Later, under David Belasco's management, she trouped with Mrs. Leslie Carter in *Du Barry*, playing the young Marie Antoinette.

Mother's first glimpse of the theatre came when the nuns took her French class to see Sarah Bernhardt in *Phèdre*. "I thought she was all glory then; she was bewitching; she played like the most extraordinary violin." A dozen years later my mother was engaged to walk on with La Grande Sarah in scenes from her famous plays. Seeing the world's most celebrated actress at close range gave Mother sharp reservations. "How she ranted in that silver-sweet voice of hers! And those fingers — painted scarlet straight to the first knuckle!"

Her memory was erratic after World War II, but Mother clearly recalled "walking out with a very young man named James Joyce." She met him, I believe, when the Benson company visited Dublin and "the perfect gentleman" invited her to a lecture on Ibsen and one day took her out in a punt. "He was writing poetry and stories of Dublin life. No one would publish them," she said, "but he used to read them in fashionable drawing rooms." What was he like as a person? "Never an unseemly word passed from his lips. He was dreadfully conceited, dapper and a bit of a dandy, but his manner was ever courteous — a true artist." James Joyce introduced her to the plays of Ibsen: "Oh, I took a great fancy to them, especially *The Lady from the Sea*. But after I married your father Ibsen did seem such nonsense to me."

Not until my adolescence did I discover that my mother was

unconsciously adding delicate tints and shades to everything she did: every object she touched was picked up or set down with a certain grace, as if she were on stage. In my childhood Mother enjoyed the role of Lovely Lady and since she was quite unaware that she was acting in real life, she was extremely effective.

Father was often called "Judge," an accurate though misleading title — he was judge of the horse races. I had not seen my father on the grandstand until some years after the war when he appeared suddenly in close-up, in a newsreel of prewar Manila. Easy-going and optimistic, my father possessed all the virtues — and limitations — to be found in Kipling's "If" or Polonius' advice to his son.

Infected by the American expansionist fever during the Spanish-American War, Father was cured when he saw the ruthless repression of the Filipino in the desperate Philippine-American War that raged for two years afterwards. He rarely referred to the controversies of his times, and yet when reactionary men railed against Philippine independence, he calmy spoke in its favor. If his attitude was tinged with paternalism, his deep-rooted love of the Filipinos and their traditions and customs was stronger. Manila was his home: he had severed his ties with the United States and visited the land of his birth only three times in his long life.

When I arrived on the scene, Papa was fifty-five and no longer the dashing man about town of his early photographs. There was a sedate, old-world charm about him, his vintage being as distinctly pre–World War I as his New Year's Eve champagne — Pommery & Greno, 1911. Unlike the old colonialists, Father did not wear a pith helmet; he wore a smart straw hat. He dressed in white linen suits (a clean one twice a day), wore brocade neckties from Hong Kong and jade sleeve-links, and carried his walking stick with the air of a Spanish don. As the playwright Severino Montano wrote me from Manila, Father's ways seemed "more Continental than those of a pioneering Californian."

During the great earthquake of 1937, I remember how Father sat me up on his lap, showing me his engraved gold pocket watch and its chain of golden nuggets from the Benguet Mines in Baguio. While the house heaved about us, I sat on my papa's knee, studying the roman numerals of his watch and, with his arms around me, I was not in the least afraid of the convulsions in the earth.

In the Escolta, the heart of Manila's business district, stood a familiar landmark often seen on post cards before the war. It was a two-storey building with a plain white-lettered sign:

F. W. PRISING, TOBACCO PRODUCTS.

I knew nothing of my father's business except that he supplied Manila cigars to the ships that sailed into the bay. On sunny Saturday afternoons I rushed down to the crags of the breakwater at my father's heels and he pointed out cargo boats in quarantine, gunboats that lay at their buoys and merchant ships steaming in and out of Manila Bay. Father knew every ship by name. Standing in the dim rainbow of the salt sea spray, he identified vessels of the old Dollar Line (actual big dollar signs on their funnels), the dreadnought *Prince of Wales* en route to Singapore, the German *Scharnhorst* and all manner of tramps, colliers, tankers bound for Mombasa and Bombay, Auckland and Liverpool, Suribaya and San Francisco. This was the heyday of the great passenger ships. Nothing could eclipse them; neither the German Zeppelin nor the American airship, the *China Clipper,* that alighted on pontoons on the choppy sea. But of the many steamships that sailed into Manila Bay I considered one my own: the stately *Empress of Japan,* which towered like a white castle on the hills of the waves. Between 1933 and 1939 I made seven voyages in the *Empress of Japan,* and often if I were not aboard I was out to watch her tugged to her moorings at Manila's Pier Seven, the longest pier in the world.

The Empress of Japan

EXCITEMENT OF DEPARTURE: sharp whistles, a hustle of stewards and passengers, the great gasps of the ship's horn. Father would put Mother and me into our stateroom with my portable gramophone, our luggage and steamer rugs. At the last gong he would leave us on deck and stand on the pier waving us off to the brassy strains of "Over the Bounding Main." Then, with the final blasts of the horn, the hawsers were released and I could feel the great ship pull free. And I would scramble up to the boat deck as the *Empress of Japan* sailed past the rock fortress of Corregidor and out into the South China Sea. I studied the ship from stem to stern, harassed the seamen who swabbed the decks, and inspected the engine room; and whenever I was exhausted by these explorations, I sat beside my mother in my deck chair sipping beef tea while she pored over some anthology by Somerset Maugham. We were good sailors both: when the sea went rough and the crew battened down for a storm, we kept to the deck and regarded with pitiless scorn all less seasoned travellers who tottered to their cabins with queasy looks and a bruised color under their eyes.

Elegance, and not mere luxury, was still in vogue during those closing days of colonialism and privilege. Everyone dressed for dinner, Mother in her classic Grecian gowns by Mariano Fortuni of Venice. Passengers glanced at the mysterious lady who smiled and exchanged pleasantries with them and who frequently won at the ship's lottery. No one guessed that she had been on the stage; and nosey parkers who questioned the purser were surprised to discover that she was a tobacco merchant's wife.

To me, a trip in the *Empress* was a perpetual pleasure round of games, films, lotteries, the ship's concert, the Captain's dinner (when grown-ups looked foolish blowing squeakers and wearing paper hats); and at the stops along the way, I tossed streamers of pink and blue from the great white *Empress* to the shore.

But the gangway of the luxury liner led down to the discovery of poverty and squalor at every port. They stood out more starkly by contrast. All the poverty I saw in the 1930s was of the Orient — beggars, rickshaw boys, coolies, women coaling ships or building roads followed by their hungry, half-naked children with bloated bellies and match-stick legs. Poverty for them was not an accident of the depression or a temporary misfortune; it was their only way of life. And they bore it like dumb beasts of burden from their births to their early deaths. A coolie, for example, had a life expectancy of eight years once he became a rickshaw runner. Life is cheap in Asia, people said. I felt, looking upon the poor, as if I were seeing a different species. I was sorry for them, just as I was sorry when I saw cruelty practiced on animals, a coachman whipping his horse. One could interfere, however, when animals were mistreated, as Father did when he ordered a coachman to stop abusing his horse. Human misery seemed even more remote. Not until the war did I realize that whatever happened to any man could also happen to me.

2.

Shanghai was a city of crisis, a city living at the brink of catastrophe. Warships of six nations patrolled the Whangpu and Yangtze rivers; a dozen of them lay at anchor in full view of the Bund, waiting for an incident. Apart from the French and British colonialists, the city was filled with distressed cargo: impoverished Chinese refugees from Nanking, Russians who had fled the Bolshevik revolution or Stalin's purges. There were scores of bag-snatchers, prostitutes, gangsters and drunken sailors. Although I understood little of what I saw, the atmosphere slowly worked its impact into me. Trotting along in a rickshaw just off Foochow Road, Mother and I passed the child prostitutes. In cheap green frocks, their lips smeared with rouge and their swollen eyelids with kohl, young girls scarcely older than ten or twelve slunk in doorways like emaciated child corpses, chatting and smoking cigarettes. "Those are very bad girls," Mother sadly murmured, "but they must work so hard for a living."

When we stopped, the coolie carefully lifted me out of the rickshaw and left the imprint of his filthy hands on my white sailor suit. I cannot forget the waves of embarrassment, the disgust and the pity that rose up in me or the dim feeling that his handprints were an accusation.

The *Empress* was about to sail from Shanghai. We were up on the embarkation deck caught in the press of passengers who were giving last-minute gifts, babbling "Chin-chin" and "Toodleloo" and "Do give my love to cousin Bertie," when a pasty-faced Chinese woman with a baby wrapped up in a shawl came up to Mother.

"Missie, you wantchee buy'em girl baby — yes? Only five dollar U.S. Buy'em cheap — very cheap."

Obviously ill, the woman became hysterical when Mother refused to buy the baby.

"Aw no — not you, Missie. You got muchee money; you go buy this baby and you buy'em many baby with muchee money more."

Ship's gongs were ringing; the stewards were calling "All ashore." Mother had given some money to the Chinese woman who kept trying to thrust the infant into Mother's arms. Tears blotched the woman's rice-powdered face; the baby was crying in the shawl.

"Quickie, Missie. You take 'em baby. Quickie."

By this time Mother was thoroughly rattled and could only summon a ship's officer who, with several cabin boys, hustled the Chinese woman and her baby down the gangway. "They don't want the girl children," a clergyman was saying. "Only the boys." For several years afterwards I believed that this was how parents got their children: they bought them, though no doubt the better children were picked out at a proper shop, a hospital or something.

3.

Mother and I arrived in Canada the first week of June 1939. We left the *Empress of Japan* at Vancouver, the city of my birth, on a bright, clear day. Everything in the city was sparkling and clean, the population bustled with excitement, many of the buildings were freshly painted in preparation for the visit of the king and queen. We were soon dashing through the Rockies in a train bound for the East. Each town that we passed shone in the sharp sunlight, trimmed for a festival; every station on the line to Toronto was decked with bunting, flags and flowers; bands rehearsed on the platforms to welcome the royal family.

In Toronto I was put to board at the Epsom School. Mother left for New York, where Grandmother lived on Long Island. Granny, I was told, had become very old and very ill and Mother was going to take care of her. I had never been left to stay with strangers.

The Epsom School had closed for the summer, so I was the only boarder. Everyone was on holiday except Mrs. Epsom and the maid. A white-haired widow of sixty, Mrs. Epsom was chinless; she had a pear-shaped figure and cultivated pear-shaped tones. Her white hair was marcelled, a peculiar form of regimented waves not uncommon to older women in the 1930s; I thought she was wearing a wig. Mrs. Epsom's mouth was small, pink and prudish — her teeth reminded me of mice.

Mrs. Epsom had determined to turn me into a "gentleman" — a word which she rolled on her tongue as if tasting a mint. At our first supper she cooed, "Ilboos off the table!" Next morning she seemed unduly inquisitive and anxiously enquired whether I had done Big Archie and Little Archie directly after breakfast.

"Are you quite sure you *flushed* Big Archie and Little Archie down the toilet, dear?"

I thought, for some misguided reason, that Mrs. Epsom spoke of tadpoles and frogs.

I was sent to bed in broad daylight. Mrs. Epsom would step into my room to supervise my evening prayers. She made her enquiries the first night:

"And now, dear, what are the prayers you say with mummy ivery night?"

"God-bless-mummy-and-daddy-and-granny-and-allmyfriends-amen."

"Lovely, quite lovely, and of course we'll say that one too, but we must say others. Don't you know the Lord's Prayer?"

"Yes, Mummy always recites it."

"One doesn't *recite* prayers, dear; one *says* them. And I've got such a nice little *new* one for you. Come along, say it after me:

> Now I lay me down to sleep;
> I pray the Lord my soul to keep.
> If I should die before I wake,
> I pray the Lord my soul to take."

After prayers, Mrs. Epsom tucked me up too tightly, pecked my cheek and departed on tiptoe, shutting the door behind her. I would kick off the bedclothes and lie awake waiting for the night to fall. "If I should die before I wake" kept repeating itself in my mind. Only very old people died; indeed that must

be a prayer for very old people to recite. I would think of
Granny — she was very, very old. And as the night shadows crept
into the room, I would go to my window and wait for the stars.

Mrs. Epsom used to read Mother's letters to me, just before I
went to bed. One night Mrs. Epsom came in and whispered,
"Mummy's letter is going to be somewhat hard for you to understand, dear. You do *know* where Mummy *is,* don't you?"

"With Granny." "If I should die before I wake" came to me
in a flash. "Mama's letter says that Gran died, doesn't it?"

"Whatever do you mean?" Mrs. Epsom asked, pursing her
lips.

The letter said: "Your ever-loving Granny passed high into
heaven yesterday."

That night I waited a long time before the shadows came.
I remembered how, when I was three, we had stayed with
Granny at her white Colonial farmhouse with its pillared porch
and its apple and peach orchards. Papa had bought the farm in
East Setauket when he married Mother. Gran told me of
Bristol, where she was born, of the Clifton Downs, of ships that
came in from Cardiff and of her Grandfather Nelson who had
been a lamplighter and lit the lamps of Bristol. I wanted to
go to Bristol to see the lighting of the lamps, but Granny
smiled, "Oh no, not anymore. It's all changed now. One man
pulls a switch and they all come on."

I brought my chair over to the window and gazed down the
street at the maple trees. Darkness began to fall. All at once
the lamps in the street flicked on. I thought of Granny and her
Grandfather Nelson. The bright street lamps put out my fear
of the dark. I knew that one day I would die, when I was very
old like Granny; but she was eighty and I was only six. I could
count my years with one hand and a finger and yet Granny was
so old that her age couldn't be counted, not even on fingers
and toes.

Towards the end of August Mrs. Epsom began preparing to

open her school, and when she was not interviewing applicants I was permitted to look through magazines in what she called the parlor or to listen to the wireless. Voices on the radio kept mentioning Hitler and the words "dictator," "Nazi" and "Danzig." Mrs. Epsom kept saying, "He'd never dare!"

Hitler had a very nasty name; it sounded as if he were always striking people. I had heard it first the year before. We had gone down to Pier Seven in Manila to see the ballet-mistress off in the *Scharnhorst* — this was soon after the Anschluss, when Hitler rode through the streets of Vienna. The band at the pier was playing a waltz and the Viennese ballet-mistress was weeping. "Do you know what they are playing?" she had asked. " '*Wiener Blut*' — 'Vienna Blood.' "

Before bedtime when I had washed, scrubbed my teeth and dutifully flushed Big Archie and Little Archie down the toilet, Mrs. Epsom called to me up the stairs.

"Comb your hair, dear, and put on your dressing gown and slippers; then come down to the parlor."

As I entered the sitting room I noticed that the light was on in the wireless. The maid was standing grimly beside it.

"Britain is at war," Mrs. Epsom announced. "You shall hear your king speak tonight. We must stand up straight for his speech."

Through the wheeze and crackle of static, a man who seemed to have a bad cold made a halting speech. Summer was over. It was September 1939.

Mother arrived the morning after war was declared and she looked extremely chic. Dressed entirely in black, she was mourning for Granny in a stylish coat and turban of moiré antique. A black fox curled round her throat, biting its tail. The moment she sat down in the Epsom parlor I said that I detested the place and wished to leave at once. This spoilt the pretty scene. Mother flew into a temper and, with a souvenir cane from the New York World's Fair, she took me out to the porch and cried, "I'll make you dance." The cane stung my legs as I trotted up and down trying to skip the blows.

When the dancing lesson was over we rushed to the train for New York. I was so enraged at my mother that I refused to speak until she broke the cane to bits before the train reached Buffalo.

We stayed the week in New York with Violet Heming, a friend of Mother's from her theatre days. Auntie Vi was fresh from her comedy success in *Yes, My Darling Daughter,* and in real life she did seem to have stepped out of the latest drawing-room comedy, with her puns and quips, her blue sparkling eyes, and her sophisticated Mayfair manner. She refused to be intimidated by a six-year-old boy who was impressed with having seen her on the screen in *The Man Who Played God.* The film stars George Arliss (my father's favorite actor); Violet Heming is the leading lady and young Bette Davis the ingenue. When Auntie Vi married Senator Bennett Champ Clark after the war, President Truman was best man. I am uncertain whether the best man or the groom was leading man at the wedding — Violet Heming decidedly remained the leading lady. But whenever I remember that autumn of 1939, I see her hiding a tiny bottle of champagne in my pocket as she put my mother and me into the train back to Canada.

4.

In early summer our trip across Canada had been favored by fair skies, and festive crowds waited at station platforms to cheer the king and queen. On our return the skies remained fair and the platforms still crowded, but the air had turned cold — the festival was over. All the way west, at every station, troops hung out of the windows of trains bound for the East. The same bands that welcomed King George VI were playing the soldiers off to war. Women packed the station platforms and hugged their men who leaned from the windows of departing trains. At one station, near Winnipeg, as the train began to move, a grey-haired woman still clung to her son, weeping savagely. The train dragged her the full length of the platform until she fell by the track. The waving women at the station screamed, their wild smiles vanishing, but when they went to help the old woman up, she rose of her own accord and stood cursing the crowd.

On our return to Vancouver, Mother took me to St. Paul's Hospital, where I had been born. The doctors, the nurses, and the Sisters of Providence gathered round me, praising my mother, exclaiming at how fortunate I was, expressing surprise that I had grown into such a healthy and handsome young lad. With vague misgivings, I realized that there had been something unusual about my birth. But my curiosity did not linger on the subject; a taxi piled with all our luggage was waiting for us, ready to take us to the ship. Transports loaded with soldiers lay at the Vancouver docks like carcasses thick with flies. Our once-white *Empress of Japan* had come down from the Esquimalt graving dock painted battleship-grey and armed with anti-aircraft guns at her stern.

5.

Five days later we were ashore at Honolulu for the day. At sailing time, the pier was hectic with hula girls singing "Aloha" as streamers fluttered and stretched from our grey, armed ship to their habitual gaiety. While missionaries primmed their lips and boozy tourists snapped cameras, the *Empress of Japan* broke the last flimsy strands of streamers that bound her to the Hawaiian shore. Twilight rapidly darkened over Pearl Harbor; apprehension was growing aboard ship because we were bound next for Yokohama. Japan was in sympathy with the Fascist powers and although she was not yet at war it meant that our next three ports of call would be less than neutral.

Up on the promenade deck after early breakfast, Mother and

I were surveying the tiny green islands of Yokohama Bay. "Look! there's the *Scharnhorst!*" I called, stirring a rustle of excitement among the other passengers who refused to believe me. My friend, the purser, trim and efficient in white uniform, stepped by. "That's the *Scharnhorst,* surely," he confirmed. "No trouble, though — she's not armed. She was beyond the three-mile limit when we sighted her. But she's well into Japanese waters by now." I peered through the pearl-handled opera glasses, starboard towards Fujiyama in the distance, and as we passed alongside the German liner, my view was obstructed. On the intruder's mast I saw the black, encircled swastika of the Nazi flag.

Not until we docked at Kobe, however, did I see the unmistakable signs of militarist Japan. As our ship was mooring, I popped my head out of our porthole and noticed a troop of Japanese boys, scarcely older than myself, marching with rifles almost as tall as the lads themselves. They were drilled up and down the quay — as if to impress tourists — by a brisk, blustering sergeant.

A typhoon warning was up at Nagasaki, our last Japanese port, and at our departure the dock coolies were dressed in palm-leaf raincoats. Outward bound for Shanghai, we made for the open sea, skirting the edge of the storm. Splashed by rain, I stood at the deckhouse astern of the *Empress of Japan,* gazing at the ship's wake as she shook in the swing of the waves. Then when I glanced up to look back at that city of shipyards, Christian missions, bridges humped over myriad canals and homes built high into the hills, I saw Nagasaki half-shrouded by surging black clouds.

Big Ching rang seven times from the tower of the Customs Building on the Bund. And there at the jetty was Adeline Mumby, flaunting a fedora at a raffish angle, making her jaunty salute as she welcomed us to Shanghai. During supper at the Metropole, Miss Mumby declared that she had no intention of leaving China. "War? Oh, maskee," said she, employing a word from pidgin, so dear to old colonialists, meaning "never mind." "Besides," she continued, flicking spilt cigarette ash from her cravat, "I've a smart new flat in Avenue Edward the Seventh, so now I'm a proper Shanghailander." During the Great War, she told us, she had driven an ambulance in Belgium. "Wanted to get into the thick of the fighting. Face to face with the Hun, don't y'know? Just what I did, too. *And* got out without a scratch!" Miss Mumby filled her glass brimful with wine and set off reminiscing about her chequered career, which proved quite an education for me. Prison, I had always thought, was a place only for criminals until I learnt that Adeline Mumby had been jailed for a fortnight. "Jolly interesting place to be, Holloway Prison," she said with a defiant jut of her chin. "Women wouldn't vote today if I'd not been there!" She punctuated this boast with a superb drop of her monocle. Then, lifting her glass, she tossed off the last of her wine, smartly. Her gesture bore the mark of finality: supper was over and we never saw intrepid Miss Mumby again.

Shanghai, in my childhood, was divided into colonial concessions. The next day, an hour before sailing time, Mother and I visited the garden near the British consulate in the international settlement. We entered, as I remember, by means of a small coin in a turnstile. It was a mildly warm, breezy morning. Petulant, genteel ladies in walking-dress and stiff, starchy gentlemen stepped among the flowers, raising parasols. I was beginning to read at the time and noticed a discreet sign placed before some shrubbery. "Dogs" it began, which immediately roused my attention. "Dogs and —" but I could not read what followed. Mother flushed and refused to read it to me, but I insisted. The notice was rather rude, she said, and most unkind:

Dogs and Orientals Not Allowed.

A Home by the Sea

1

IN FEBRUARY 1941, ten months before the start of the Pacific war, the wives and children of American military personnel were ordered to leave the Philippines and return to the United States. But my parents paid little attention to the movements of troops or their families. Father and Mother and I had moved out to live just south of Manila, to immense rambling gardens by the sea. Here, safe from the primitive jungle which stretched beyond, I grew to the age of eight, as carefully tended as the bougainvillea and oleander that spread their reckless patterns down to the shore.

With our new home, a tall, handsome fellow called Looming entered my life. He was not the sort of chap I could easily imagine in such workaday roles as gardener and chauffeur; he looked more like a guide who could slash down trails through the jungle. His face was oblong with lank, blue-black hair slanting over his eyes, and he wore a red hibiscus tucked close to his ear. We made friends at once. Actually, Looming himself was proud of his skill as a gardener: he taught me the names of the flowers, showed me the orchids potted in coconut husks hanging from the banyan tree and, in his soft sensual voice, told me that at night, when the flame trees flickered with fireflies, the night-blooming *dama de noche*, lady of the night, would pervade the garden with her perfume. In this same cool garden of moss and grass, with its pond of goldfish and water lilies forever shaded by the rooting, spreading banyan tree, Looming and I fed the black and white rabbits with lettuce leaves. Wild monkeys went swinging on their tails from bough to bough of the banyan tree and pelted us with rinds and seeds. Out in the large, hot gardens where grew the yellow blood-flecked lily, Spanish flag, Looming and I shaded our eyes with our hands as we gazed up at the aeroplanes flying over our gardens to Nichols Field, the military airport hardly a kilometre away.

Far from the Nazi invasion of Europe and the Battle of Britain, our life by the sea was a two-year idyl in the glad sun's light. Mother began collecting all kinds of pets and giving them absurd names. Besides the rabbits and the monkeys, we had Smoky Moonlight, a vain Persian tabby, Jill, the wire-haired terrier and, of course, Napoleon, the cockatoo of my earliest memories. Presently Snow came to join us — an amazing white cat the size of an ocelot. He was ash-grey when he arrived and was christened after he emerged pure white from a bath. Snow was an exceptional cat bred by Mrs. MacFarren, who crossed large Siamese temple cats with Angoras and produced huge, smooth-haired, white felines with eccentric dispositions. Feline, for example, Snow refused to be. He was a dog in cat's clothing who romped about with terrier Jill and enjoyed a good roll in the mud.

My first personal dog was Sally. While I was at my lessons on the verandah with my tutor, Miss Jane, I heard the telephone ring and Mother's voice fluting its distinct tones from low to high to low again: "Yes, I will take Sally." That evening, when Looming brought my father home, they were accompanied by a black cocker spaniel with exceptionally lugubrious eyes.

"She's called Sally after the poem, 'Sally in Our Alley' — for she's a silly Sally"; but not even Mother's silvery syllables could justify that name!

Sally nuzzled me; she followed me wherever I went. I brushed her daily and took her swimming in the sea. During the war, the very thought of Sally, with her ridiculously sentimental name, broke me to tears. I was fully fourteen before I could remember Sally without my throat tightening with the pain of the past.

Two large compounds lay next to ours, one some distance along the shore, the other behind our garden, where some Dutch people lived. Adjacent to the Dutch compound, in a clearing in the jungly wood, stood a Filipino barrio of less than a dozen bamboo huts on stilts. Mine was a hedged-in paradise: I yearned to discover the world beyond. At first I merely parted the leaves in a thicket of bamboo and peered at the Filipina women cooking over a clay-pot stove, and once on a feast day I watched the roasting of a pig on a spit over an open fire. On Saturdays I had seen the men and boys squat round in a circle, placing bets and shouting excitedly during a cock fight.

Looming told me that in this particular barrio, after a cock fight, a husband had caught his wife with another man and he pitched a dead, blood-drenched rooster on his wife's naked belly. For some reason, this frightened her lover away. Intrigued by Looming's tale, I sensed that I might learn about matters my parents never mentioned and wandered one day into the barrio with a beating heart and glittering eyes. The barrio folk gathered round me, and while I stood there a smiling fool, they wagged their fingers and shook their heads as an old Filipina grandmother climbed backwards down the bamboo steps of a nipa hut and led me firmly by the wrist, repeating in English and Tagalog, "Bad boy. Go home. Go."

When Terray got married I could not understand why she had not married Alfredo. Indeed the very idea of Alfredo and marriage convulsed her with giggles. Mother put an end to my questioning. "Alfredo is not the marrying sort," she replied,

and she and Terray went on sewing costumes for Mother's production of *The Trojan Women.* Terray loved costumes and
the theatre and attended all the dress rehearsals with me. In
addition to accompanying me on such outings, Terray insisted
upon tying my shoes since my knots refused to become properly
square. This was a major humiliation for me and one that I
hoped was kept secret from Looming.

On my seventh birthday Looming presented me with a gor-
geous yellow and orange butterfly kite which he had made himself. My parents, however, disapproved of the gift — and so
strongly that I was afraid I should not be allowed to keep it.
Father was convinced that I had pestered Looming to make it
for me and my mother agreed, insisting that I certainly ought
to know that Looming had better things to do with his leisure
than make kites for me. But Looming broadly grinned at me,
flung his straight black hair off his forehead and turned his in-
fectious grin on my parents. "To make a kite is my hobby," he
said, flying the giant butterfly high over the sea and up towards
the afternoon sun. My parents were quashed by his blithe in-
sistence, of course, but later on, when Looming was not present,
they grumbled about my hanging about with a servant.

2.

Barrio life through the bamboo thicket was not my only
glimpse east of Eden, nor were my lessons with Miss Jane the
only education I received. Having discovered the pleasures of
reading with *Treasure Island,* I became addicted to the Doctor
Doolittle books and then, somewhat to my parents' bewilderment, I made an excursion into the romantic, wicked world of
Trilby. No doubt to offset the influence of life among the
artists in the Paris of 1870, I was obliged to attend a catechism
class with other children. Since I was born in a Roman Catholic
hospital and was apparently baptized Joseph, the one true

church made its claim. Mother, originally Church of England, had converted to the Church of Rome, though she dabbled from time to time in the Vedas, the Upanishads and the Bhagavad Gita.

Catechism class was taught by a little nun with some boyish and improbable name like Sister Richard Michael. Unlike some of the nuns today, Sister Richard Michael could not have been mistaken for an airline stewardess or a hospital nurse. Her black skirts were voluminous and her face peered out of a wimple. On the first day, when the class said the Lord's Prayer in unison, I continued solo with "for Thine is the Kingdom," omitted by the Romans, if not by my mother.

To prepare us for our first Holy Communion, Sister Richard Michael gave us meticulous descriptions of sin and the wages of sin. I fear that she failed to impress me with her lurid description of hell. Of purgatory she seemed to have some knowledge, yet she was obviously misinformed about heaven for she described it as being locked. Limbo, however, the doom of those lost souls, the unbaptized, filled me with dread. Very real dread. When my parents could not produce my baptismal certificate, I grew alarmed and in solemn secrecy I went to the Ermita Church, stole a bottle of holy water, waited until Alfredo had left for market and baptized myself John Joseph Julian over the kitchen sink.

My first communion passed without incident. On the day of my second communion, however, I proved an unwitting innovator. These were not the days of jazz communions and rock and roll masses: dancing, originally a form of worship, had degenerated into the brusque gestures of the priests, yet we did file into chapel. And it was in the queue to chapel that I proved an innovator by dancing the conga I had learnt on shipboard. "Agh! That's smutty! I'm going to tell Sister on you," said pious Joey behind me. And the very next day I was expelled from catechism class, having been falsely accused of dropping my plus fours and showing all the little girls and boys my round, impertinent, seven-and-a-half-year-old bare arse.

3.

Alfredo and Looming had hung every tree in the gardens with Chinese lanterns that swung in the breeze of declining day and by nightfall flared with colored lights. Rows of cars were parked along the gravel path, and while several chauffeurs remained stiffly at their wheels reading the comics, the rest clubbed up to gamble with dice. Guests roamed through our gardens in groups and pairs, chatting and laughing, while the shadows lengthened away from the shore. Somewhere in the house a baritone was singing, "For the wind is in the palm trees an' the temple bells they say." The voice continued easily, naturally reaching a crescendo: "An' the dawn comes up like thunder outer China 'crost the bay." Then a patter of applause drifted out over the flower beds and mingled with the other sounds of the garden party.

Father and Mother stood beside each other at the verandah door, greeting guests, making introductions and small talk while Alfredo, barefooted in his white, brass-buttoned coat, moved nimbly between the verandah and sitting room, serving refreshments and drinks.

Being the only child at the party, I felt that I had managed to push my big toe into the grown-up world. Sally followed me from one group of men in tropic suits and women in print party frocks to the other, eavesdropping on the tail ends of conversations. Mrs. Bunker-Hicks puffed at her Manila cigar and heaved a chesty laugh; she was leaving by clipper for San Francisco; no, she was not afraid of flying; she had settled her affairs; it was time to get out. Meanwhile, the monkeys up in their banyan tree were silent, but they too must have overheard the visitors exchanging current Manila gossip and the East-Asian war rumors of November 1941.

Ever since Mother and I had returned to Manila at the out-break of war in Europe, all news was bad news. Over our black short-wave radio came word of the retreat from Dunkirk and the fall of Paris, and then obscure, censored reports of the Battle of Britain. Often I imagined that I could hear the Japanese guns in China but my parents, having lived so long in the Orient, had grown accustomed to what they called "China trouble." Two years after my father went out to the Far East there had been the Boxer Rebellion. He spoke of the constant strife in China — "the '27 trouble" and "the '32 trouble"; even I could remember "the '37 trouble." Ah, well, maskee, my parents would say; Manila was separated from China by the sea and with invulnerable Corregidor guarding Manila Bay, our lives and home were safe. Whenever I asked my father if there would be a war with Japan, he took down the big atlas and showed me the map of China, a nation so vast and populous, he assured me, that it would simply absorb the Japanese armies for a century.

But the signs were plain. Driving home at dusk we saw the shapes of tanks and heavy guns beneath camouflage tarpaulin, the latest shipments from the United States. General Mac-Arthur had launched a crash program for the defense of the Philippine archipelago; he was building up and training the Filipino forces and expected them to be prepared by April of 1942.

In July 1941, when the Japanese occupied southern Indo-China, the United States promptly severed trade relations with Japan. This was, in effect, an ultimatum. With the trade waters of South-East Asia closed to the Japanese, their economy was severely threatened. If the Japanese were going to strike out in South-East Asia they would have to do so before the Philippine defense program was completed, before MacArthur's deadline of April 1942.

In the meantime most American civilians in the Philippines were half-asleep; like my father they had settled down to their homes in this far outpost of American altruistic expansionism. And when threats of war did cross their minds, they reassured themselves that the United States was very big and Japan very small — the leisurely life under the Philippine sun was not conducive to fear — and the tropic breezes lulled them back to their siesta.

The first turn in our slumber had nothing directly to do with the impending war. A new law required all aliens in the Philippine Commonwealth to register. This alerted us to the fact that I, having been born in Canada, was an alien with a British passport. Mother, on the other hand, was an American by marriage. She was never quite conscious of her citizenship until she was obliged to stand in a separate queue with me while I was registered. To Mother passports were a nasty nuisance and, anyway, in her youth, before the Great War, when the world was still civilized, one did not hear of passports.

Not until late October, when General Tojo became premier of Japan, did my parents grow genuinely alarmed. Father decided that Mother and I should leave after the Christmas holidays and he booked our passage aboard the *President Polk,* bound for San Francisco in January of 1942. Now that Tojo and the military extremists ruled Japan, the nasality of newscasters grew louder in our home than the sweet tone of Fritz Kreisler on my gramophone.

My parents, like most people in any age, had a very intermittent grasp of political realities. They were shocked to hear of wars and diplomatic blunders. But what, after all, could one do? Even in democracies the vote is often a delusion of personal influence; rarely, in fact, does one have the opportunity to choose between the lesser of several evils. Yet my parents were too Victorian to be cynical, so they paid their taxes, tossed up their hands in genteel despair at governments, crooks and politicians and settled back into their private lives. In our home by the sea we tossed aside the gloomy rumors of war and settled down to saving the life of a tiny black kitten.

We had cured Blackie's sick eyes and rickets. In two months she had grown sleek and strong, and made a habit of hopping up on the conch shells which decorated the verandah steps. She used the biggest shell at the topmost step as a sort of seesaw, merrily teeter-tottering on it, clawing. Quite suddenly, as I watched her at this game one morning, the shell dislodged and, with Blackie's claws hooked to it, the great conch rolled under and over, down the thirteen tiled steps, crushing the kitten as it went. Hardly able to move, I stood there calling my mother to the verandah. Blackie had freed herself from the shell and, bolting up the steps, the kitten made a flying leap to my mother's breast, catching its tiny claws into her dress. A quick gasp; blood trickled from the kitten's nose; then its body went limp with the claws still clinging to my mother's dress. Blackie was dead.

But I would not believe it. How could she be dead if her eyes were open?

Mother freed the kitten's claws from her dress, speaking softly.

"Her breath has stopped. She is dead and gone now, dead and gone."

"No, Mother, her eyes are wide open."

The kitten's head sagged. Those wide blue eyes no longer blinked. Only then would I believe that the creature that frisked with life scarcely five minutes ago was a mere bit of black fur with dead, staring eyes.

Snuffling up my tears, I heard the smack of Looming's spade digging the grave in the garden. Mother had taken an old chocolate box and lined it with satin.

"But she won't be able to breathe in that box, Mother!"

"Fetch her some flowers, pretty ones; there's a good lad."

And I went out fetching fistfuls of tiny pinks and whites and brought them to the grave beside the oleander at the foot of the steps, close to the place where the kitten had been crushed.

As we laid the chocolate box in the earth, it was so full of black fur and flowers that it would not close.

That weekend the ships in Manila Bay were in blackout at night; air-raid sirens practiced during the day. Soon afterwards Father came home for lunch and we took the red glass and the blue glass bowls out of their silver jam pots and stood by the flowering bush of poisonous oleander — Father, Mother, Miss Jane and I — gazing through glass bowls as the sun was eclipsed.

11

Children Are Never Told

Business As Usual

DRESSED UP in my white sailor suit, I go into Mother's room to find her sitting before her dressing table. She has just noticed the first strand of grey in her hair and, smiling faintly, she plucks it out by the root. Although she admits to being in her mid-fifties, her face is not marked by her age — at a guess, she might pass for forty-six. Dabbling her little finger in a pot of pale rouge, she brushes her lips quickly, secretively, and then wipes most of it off. In 1941 she wears no more make-up than she did as a young woman.

In Manila, across the international dateline, today is Monday, December eighth — the Feast of the Blessed Virgin — though in the other half of the world it is still December seventh. Mother and I are going to mass at Our Lady of Lourdes in Intramuros, Manila's Walled City established by Spaniards in the sixteenth century. I watch her pick up the black lace veil which lies neatly folded on top of her Church of England Book of Common Prayer. Mother has always gone to Roman mass with an Anglican prayer book.

On the longish trip to Intramuros, Looming drives us down the sedate Dewey Boulevard with its fine mansions and villas, past the El Nido where Father's friend Mr. Perkins lives in a Moorish castle guarded by turbaned Sikhs, past embassies and consulates, past the American high commissioner's residence, and the Bay View Hotel, all of them looking out over Manila Bay towards Corregidor. The tropical December day is so hot and stifling that steam seems to rise from the strip of road before us.

"Why, everyone must be at church," Mother remarks, surprised. Indeed, the Boulevard is unaccountably deserted for midmorning. Usually at this hour the Chinese amahs in white coolie shirts and black silk trousers would be sitting round in circles on the green, prattling away in singsong Cantonese. Protected within the singing circles of amahs, toddlers would be playing together, squabbling over spades and pails.

Mother is in a comfortable, mildly talkative mood and as the car swings round the Luneta, she tells me that this grassy park and promenade (where in moonlight Colonel Loving leads his military band) had in earlier years been a vast swamp of cobras and malaria mosquitoes. Presently we pass along the clipped sward of the golf links, which for three centuries of Spanish rule was the treacherous moat of crocodiles that surrounded the black stone walls and bastions of Intramuros. As we approach the gates of the ancient city, Mother's voice lilts into its bedtime story tone: Seven gates led through these ancient walls of stone. Through the Royal Gate only the Spanish governor and the papal nuncio passed. The Parian Gate opened into the Chinese market, the Isabella Gate led to the boats on the Pasig River, but through the San Carlos Gate Filipino patriots were led in manacles and chains, prisoners on their way to the dungeons of Fort Santiago.

Once within the walls we thread our way through the maze of cobbled streets, passing the governor's palace, the immense Ionic and Corinthian San Agustín Church, the medieval courtyards with their arches and flowered balconies. We see the craftsmen carving wooden images of saints, the blacksmith nailing a shoe to a horse. In this citadel of Romanesque and baroque architecture, where urchins play in the narrow alleys and beggars sit in the sun, life goes on much as it did over a

century ago. Trotting up and down the streets are horse carriages, smartly painted red, green or blue. Our square, large
Chrysler limousine is the only intrusion of modern times. As
we approach the church of Nuestra Señora de Lourdes, a great
cart of sacks is being pulled by a patient carabao, water buffalo,
slowly, laboriously in the overpowering sun.

We are late. High Mass is already in session in the slim white
and silver rococo church; the kneeling throng is exceptionally
hushed — even for fervent Manila Catholics. Three chanting
priests weave back and forth at the altar, while behind them
their acolytes ring bells and swing censers of heady, fuming in-
cense. Throughout the mass I am mesmerized by the smoky,
grey-blue spirals wafting up towards the crystal chandeliers lit
with flickering tapers. Hot, dripping tallow and the odor of
nard. In the thick silence which weighs so heavily over the confines of the church, this feast day mass resembles a Lenten service
or requiem for the dead. Neither the chants of the priests, the
silver bells, the mumbled prayers nor a parishioner's echoing
cough can pierce this oppressive stillness until, at the Ave Maria
after the mass, the congregation's abrupt refrain shatters the
silence like a volley of shots.

Out once more into the blaze of white heat and back into the
car. Looming turns from the sixteenth-century Intramuros and
over to the nineteenth-century and modern Manila, heading
for Calle Apollinario Mabini. The crowds on the sultry pavements walk in confused patterns; their pace quickens and slows
like the gait of lost dogs. Sitting taut on the grey whipcord up-
holstery of our car, I sense an unfamiliar anxiety in the street.
The babble of voices is muffled by the thick plate-glass windows.
People stand in long queues before the food shops: some are
making fitful, clumsy gestures; others look sullen and dazed as
they wait in the glaring noon.

We step out of the car and Looming drives off. Instantly
Mother and I are swept up into the confusion of the crowd, our
errands forgotten. Passersby mutter to themselves; their eyes are

glazed, their faces tight. The only person we recognize is old Margaret Enright coming out of a shop several doors down the street. Clasping her hands and raising them over her head she cries out to us, "It can't be true! It simply can't be true!"

My mother goes over to kiss her and Mrs. Enright is telling her something that I cannot hear. At once Mother's voice turns to ice. "Perfect nonsense, Margaret. Rumors. Nothing but rumors, my dear." She brushes the little old lady aside like a bothersome fly. "I shan't listen to silly stories," Mother says crossly and refuses to answer my question as we make our way through the crush of the crowd. I listen to the voices about me, catching only a word or a phrase here and there, trying to fit them together:

> Hit
> Roosevelt
> this morning
> battleships
> two waves
> radio

At the street corner, around a telephone pole, a knot of boys jabber excitedly. The boys are making sounds of aeroplanes and explosions.

"What's the matter? What's happened?" I call to them.

"Bomba! BOMBA!" they shout.

Breaking away from my mother I rush over to them saying, "Qué pasa? Qué pasa?"

The tallest boy, his black hair falling sharply over his glasses, looks at me in amazement. Quickly his bony hands make the shape of an aeroplane.

"Los japoneses — they bombs — make bombs at Pearl Harbor. All ship — American ship — bung, bam, bim. No more ship."

"Mother — the Japanese! They've bombed Pearl Harbor!" But her reply is vague. Just behind us a man's hard, nasal voice: "And hit Clark Field — the B-17's were grounded. Tarlac, last night."

"But Mummy, Tarlac — Clark Field! They're *here* — in the Philippines."

She makes no comment. Maybe Mother has known all along and kept it from me because I am a child. "Wherever is that car?" she wonders. "Why does Looming take so long? We'd best go home by carromata."

Every horse carriage is filled. No taxis. The buses are crammed. Men are standing on the back steps of the little jitney buses. All at once a jitney stops at the corner with Father sitting in the back seat. He has already caught sight of us, his face breaking into a smile. "Don't worry! Wait for the car. I've just sent Looming back." A man jumps onto the back step, clutching the handrail as the jitney wiggles off and disappears into the traffic.

"Where's Daddy going?"

"Do stop asking questions."

The crowds along the pavement pass hurriedly by, talking loudly now. Someone says, "Not if you consider the blackout last weekend." A woman is whimpering; a big, burly American is rubbing his hands and repeating, "We're trapped in this Goddamn country. Trapped." Out of the confusion the cricket voice of an attaché at the British consulate briskly announces, "Stock up with tins, old boy, before the blitz." Through the din of Filipino, Spanish, American and Dutch voices comes the Klaxon-horn of our Chrysler limousine as Looming pulls to the curb. "Such a bobbery," Mother says as we settle ourselves into our huge home of a car. Looming starts off, hooting the traffic out of our way, and, laughing, says, "Japs can't fight Americans. All over very quick — bim-bam."

2.

War was a game. Back in our rambling gardens I could barely wait for the fun to begin. I was far too excited to imagine the actual terror and death of war. It was all great guns, something out of a story book or a costume film — Nelson at Trafalgar. I loved to dress up with a sword and eyepatch and swagger about as Nelson. It was fun to *play* at dying. I would lie on the sofa and die as Nelson: "England expects every man . . . will do . . . his duty . . . Thank God . . . I have done . . . my . . . duty . . . Kiss me, Hardy."

As a boy of eight I had seen only the death of a little black kitten. My grandmother's death, two years before, had been a disturbing but distant mystery; it set a terror in me of death in old age, of coffins and burials. The young died too, I knew, for I had recently noticed the small white hearses running their errands through the streets of Manila, carrying away white caskets with dead children. Terray should never have told me, my mother said. Looming had easily reassured me when he confirmed my parents' assertion that only very sickly children died and never healthy, happy lads like me. At any rate, I felt sure that the war would catapult me into the forbidden grown-up world where I so longed to be. If I had any qualms about the war, they gave way to the lure of the big adventure. There would be lots of noise and lots of shooting; then it would be over, as Father said, just as quickly as it had begun.

In the soft sunset, which was mellowing into dusk, I strolled with my mother down by the shore. It was silent save for the wash of the surf, but I was fairly bursting from excitement.

"There's going to be an air raid tonight!"

And Mother leaned over me in the half-light, her hair loosening in the salt sea breeze.

"No, love, there won't be an air raid," she answered quietly.

Overhead the dull motor of a reconnaissance plane flying low in the sky. It was coming towards us.

"Look up there, my pet — see! That plane will protect us."

She gestured above the black shape of a palm tree while the plane circled over us and then went westerly out to sea. Night closed down over Corregidor in the bay: the tide was in and the surf pursued us up the sand, breaking, plashing in the darkness, then slapped at my feet. The lonely little plane had turned back towards us and passed on, flicking first a red, then a green light from wing to tail fin, heading over to Nichols Field.

I woke up at midnight to a crash of kettles and pans, then a weird whine and knocking. Outside my window I could hear the jittering frenzy of monkeys in the banyan tree. The windowpanes shuddered against an explosion. Mother was already in my room, dimly visible through the white gauze of my mosquito net. I leapt out of bed: "It *is* an air raid! A *real* air raid!"

My father was standing in darkness at the door to my room, his hands cupped over a flashlight. Another blast shattered the glass in the kitchen. Father's slow voice tempered my excitement as he led me into the dining room and told me to sit quietly on the floor. When the three of us had crouched under the dining-room table, the heavy thuds and the reply of ack-ack gave way to a frustrating silence that seemed lengthened by Father's labored, asthmatic breaths.

The bombing started up again. It was louder this time and more insistent; directly overhead came a sharp nasal drone, closer and closer, until machine-gun fire drilled into our corrugated iron roof. Angrily roused, Napoleon began to shriek and flap in his covered cage. This time the whole bungalow went rocking like a ship in a typhoon, the windowpanes rattled and drummed till the glass from the dining-room window slashed across the floor. On the polished floor the smashed glass glittered in the moonlight. The next barrage shook at the house and would not stop; crack after maniacal crack split through the night — the house went on shaking. A sudden lull: in the flat zone of that silence nothing stirred; even the cockatoo had stopped. I kept straining my ears to listen. Silence. Silence. Now only a faint, absurd popping of flak and from somewhere in the vast beyond, a sickening convulsion moved in the bowels of the earth.

In time a wind rose up from the startled countryside, carrying with it an uproar of dogs, roosters and the lowing of carabaos. In the barrio nearby men were cursing, women were wailing, a child crying without check. Still we waited, huddled and sweating under the table in a circle, holding fast to each other's hands. Was the raid over? Would it start again? The wind gusted through the broken window; it was very dark; the moon had passed over. Gradually the alarms of dogs and roosters began to subside, to surrender to the night, while in the barrio the shouts and weeping dissolved into drowsy murmurs until the barrio grew quiet as cock-shut time. Far away, from some uncertain precinct in the city, the sound of the single siren died. Stillness invaded the countryside: we were left with broken glass and the dull, peaceful night.

3.

"Wrap that carefully, Terray — it's Ming! Mind the Minton, Alfredo. I'm very fond of that. Oh, and Looming, just put the silver in there; it can't break."

Last night's raid had centred on Nichols Field. In the morning the Philippine Constabulary advised civilians living near military installations to evacuate. By afternoon we were piling boxes and china and silver into the car and strapping our luggage to the roof. We had no idea of where we would go. Eventually Father rang up from his office to say that he had managed to book a room at the Leonard Wood Hotel. While Mother and I continued packing, Looming drove the first load to the hotel, took Terray to her home and brought Father home from the Escolta.

Then we were delayed by a big scene with Alfredo. Mother wept, Father stormed up and down saying that he'd never heard such damned nonsense. Alfredo refused to obey. He insisted on remaining at the house to protect it from looters. But Mother won. If Alfredo stayed, she would stay too; he began to cry and at last agreed. Father had arranged for Looming and Alfredo to sleep at the MacFarrens', near our hotel.

At sundown our 1932 Chrysler Imperial limousine rolled along the driveway, past the Dutch people's compound and out into the road. Napoleon, in his cage, sat up front between Alfredo and Looming looking, as cockatoos often do, displeased with the proceedings. Sally lay patiently in my lap while Smoky Moonlight, Mother's Persian tabby, stirred round and round in her hatbox. What would happen to Jill and Snow, I wondered. And the rabbits? What would the monkeys in the banyan tree do now?

There were no lights in the suburbs; Manila lay in total blackout as our headlights imperiously beaconed towards town. When we approached Dewey Boulevard, armed figures came into view, their rifles pointing at us. They were a squad from the Philippine Constabulary, stationed round hastily placed sandbags, prepared for an invasion. Wearing pie-plate helmets and khaki puttees (like the American troops in 1941), they looked as natty as doughboys off to the First World War.

A sergeant shouted, "What in hell are you doing with those headlights on?"

Looming craned his neck out of the window, his voice thoroughly indignant: "But this is Mr. Prising's car. We must have lights. How can we get to the town?"

"Get those Goddamn lights off or we'll shoot."

Father reached for the speaking-tube: "Looming, my boy, better put the lights out. We'll just have to creep along without them."

The Chrysler Imperial inched its way through the blackout, halted by every placement of the Constabulary.

"This is Mr. Prising's car," Looming would proudly call.

"I don't give a damn *whose* car it is," came the final reply. "Get it off the boulevard. This is WAR!"

At supper in the hotel that evening, Mother sent her curry back to the kitchen. "It's nothing but gristle," she complained to the manageress. I stole a glance at Father out of the tail of my eye. He continued calmly eating his supper and did not appear to think that Mother's behavior was, in these circumstances, in the least out of order.

We were up early next morning, after a night of distant explosions and the strident sirens, which sounded their alarm only after the bombing had begun. War or no war, Father left for his office in the Escolta. Meanwhile Mother and I went off with Looming to our seaside bungalow where two carretelas and a small, battered truck were being loaded with essential furniture. Our limousine was soon filled up with saucepans, lamps, crockery and a seventeenth-century Venetian painting of the Grand Canal; Father's long-armed teak planter's chair was roped upside down to the car's square roof. Presently the horse carts and lorry, jammed haphazard with beds, Chinese tables, and the Coromandel screen, were being led by the Chrysler in a crooked procession down the long driveway to the road. Looming was to return in an hour's time to drive us back to the hotel for lunch.

I was in the servants' quarters, directly behind the kitchen, searching for the rabbits that had fled the banyan garden, when Japanese fighter planes flew low overhead towards Nichols Field. "Mummy, come out and see — big red circles on their wings!" As I called, a Japanese Zero skimmed and dipped over the servants' yard, strafing. Bullets shot round me as I stood there looking up, shouting to my mother, telling her that I could see the pilot's head and that his cap had large, loose earflaps. All agog at the sight, I was as heedless of danger as I was deaf to my mother's shrieks. Braving the bullets, she tore down the kitchen steps, got a firm grip on me and pulled me back up into the kitchen where she gave me a good hard smack on the head. "Mind what I say — do you hear? When I call, you come!"

By now the sirens were raising the alert. We waited until we were sure there were no planes overhead. "You're going to run," said Mother, "and run you shall! Faster than you've ever run in your life. Off we go!" And we raced out into the steaming sun, across the vast length of our gardens and over to the Dutch people's compound. Here we took shelter beneath their bungalow, where they had wedged sandbags three months earlier. Our neighbors had prudently evacuated by mid-November.

The bombs began to fall soon after we had settled in the shelter. Hugging each other between the sandbags we listened to the planes roar over us. Wave upon wave of bombers drummed overhead, leaving their vibrations in the air and earth long after they had passed over to empty their bellyfuls of bombs on Nichols Field. At every lull in the bombing I wanted to run out to have a look round and Mother literally had to pin me down to keep me under cover. Although the raid continued, the strikes were no longer directed at Nichols Field, but we could hear a massive rumble of planes veering south, then heavy combustions in the distance. At last, after a long lull, sirens began the plaintive wailing of the all clear. That raid demolished the Cavité Naval Base. Over fifteen hundred men were killed.

When we emerged from the shelter we saw a fire blazing from the compound along the shore. The ground about us was sown and strewn with shrapnel; I went scouring the gardens, digging up hot, jagged bits of metal to keep for souvenirs.

The frenzied sound of a horn coming towards us. Suddenly the Chrysler came hurtling down the driveway, trailing a cloud of dust, and stopped. Looming jumped out: he was drenched in sweat, his hair dripping, his clothes pasted to his body. The moment the raid had begun he had started back to us, evading several placements of Constabulary, until he was halted by a roadblock near Nichols Field. He kept stammering over and

over, "Jesús, María, José — I think you may be dead. If anything happens, I never forgive myself. Never."

A night raid wiped out Nichols Field, the Dutch people's
house and the little barrio nearby. When Looming drove us
back, our bungalow was quietly smoldering in the bright morning sun. Only the tile steps and the verandah were still standing.
Useless to see if there was anything to salvage. We stood there
staring at our house as dumbly as strangers stare at an accident.

From beneath the verandah came a thin, timid cry. Looming
crawled under and came back with poor Snow. The cat's legs
had been mangled; he was the same color of ashes as when he
first came to us. We took him to the veterinary but I was not
allowed out of the car. When Mother and Looming returned,
I was told that, although Doctor Carlos was not in, his assistant
had promised to take good care of Snow and find him a home.
Years later, Mother told me that Snow had been chloroformed.

4.

Christmas found us still at the Leonard Wood Hotel. There
were no pageants for Mother to produce; all the schools had
been closed. In our hotel room a tiny fake Christmas tree,
dressed with tinsel and colored electric lights, stood on the desk,
Napoleon in his cage beside it. Our window was draped with a
plaid steamer rug to hide our lights during the night raids.

In former Christmases we always had a majestic Baguio pine
that reached up to the ceiling; it was decorated with real candles
and topped by a wax Danish angel with wings of lace. In the
forenoon the servants and my father's employees would gather
round the tree and, when the candles were lit, they received their
gifts: a week's wages, toys for their children, trinkets and clothing. Mother would show them the crèche with the infant Jesus,
the wise men, the shepherds and the star of Bethlehem, all made

in Germany — before 1914. Then we sang together "Joy to the World" and there would be laughter, hugging and kissing. And weeping, too, when Mother gave them her blessing and thanked them for their kindness to us. After they left, just before our Christmas dinner, I attacked the big boxes which St. Nicholas, in his jeweled bishop's mitre, had left under the tree. Nothing of prewar holidays remains, but I still have the plaid steamer rug that covered our window, as well as the box of dominoes St. Nicholas gave me that Christmas of 1941. The Brownie camera I was also given lasted through the war, only to be lost at boarding school soon after.

Hong Kong fell on Christmas Eve and General MacArthur removed his headquarters from Manila to Corregidor. Father snapped off the radio after the broadcast. The following day, however, he switched the radio on again so that we could hear President Roosevelt in a voice resonant with Christmas cheer promising us that "Help is on the way."

Great fires broke out in the Pandacan oil district; military supplies were set ablaze. Thousands of citizens were fleeing the city, for the Japanese Imperial Army had invaded our island of Luzon and by December twenty-sixth it was barely a hundred and fifty kilometres from Manila. Banks closed for the duration. Proclaiming Manila an open city, MacArthur declared that the Pearl of the Orient was of no military value and should remain safe and untouched: this, many believed, meant that it was a city through which Japanese troops might pass but which they would not occupy.

The last American aircraft that we saw proved to be the little reconnaissance plane that Mother and I had watched as we walked by the shore. While Japanese fighters and bombers flew over abandoned Manila, strafing and bombing at random, the wounded lay in the streets and the newspapers reported: Business as usual.

Open City

1.

THE DAY AFTER CHRISTMAS, we moved into a flat on the top floor of a Spanish lady's house in the Malaté district. Looming set two glass jars with Fighting Fish on my bedroom windowsill. Warning me carefully not to put both fish in a single jar, Looming explained, "Together they will fight. Then the strongest fish, he will win. But the other one, he will die." I gazed at the fish, each in its separate jar, as they nosed towards each other — behind them, the wrought-iron bars of the window. Moving swiftly, flamboyantly, the iridescent orange fish went flashing through the water in a dragon dance.

Why should they fight? Surely Looming was wrong. Both fish were well fed; even if they did quarrel, they would scarcely kill each other. They must be lonely, I thought, and if they were together, what a beautiful performance they would give.

Evening came, and bedtime. My temptation to put both fish in a single jar had grown overpowering. So I took a big spoon and lifted one of the fish out of its jar and put it in with the other. At once their ritual dance began, formal and elegant. Neither fish gave any sign of hostility; neither fish even approached the other. For more than an hour I watched the two fish swirling together.

Lulled by the rhythms of their dance, convinced by now that no harm could come, I grew drowsy and fell asleep, leaving the fish together. Next morning I woke to the cocks' crowing and the sound of sporadic shots and explosions far away. I found one of the fish floating dead at the top of the jar, while the other flared its trailing tail, still caught in its involuntary ritual, continuing its habitual dragon dance, alone.

With the Japanese Army sweeping down the Central Luzon Plain and approaching Manila, we could no longer pretend that the city would not be occupied. Through a friend at the Swiss consulate, my parents learned that the United States high commissioner had secretly fled to Corregidor, a fact that struck them as outrageous and more incredible than the advance of the Japanese. An assistant from the high commissioner's office had remained, however, and joined the Emergency Committee to advise Allied civilians in the event of an occupation. While the Japanese pushed on towards Manila by all manner of means — including a brigade on bicycles — the Committee vacillated between instructing us to congregate in one place (or several places) or to remain in our separate homes. As December drew to a close, looting broke out in the city and the last Filipino-American troops, in their retreat to Bataan and Corregidor, set off the final explosions of military supplies. We never left the house; my parents hovered fretfully over the telephone, waiting for word from the Committee, talking anxiously to friends and sifting rumors — all news was rumor now.

On New Year's Eve, when the Japanese reached the outskirts of Manila, I heard my parents talking about the Rape of Nanking. Although they refused to explain the word "rape" and evaded my questions, I could tell that this was no longer distant "China trouble." By noon Father decided that my mother and I should accept the offer of refuge from the Assumption Convent (where Mother had given an elocution class for many years) while he would return to the Leonard Wood Hotel, directly across the street from the Assumption.

Our last ride in the old Chrysler was through the convent gates. I hardly noticed Looming drive away for I was instantly distracted by the noble presence of Mother Philomene Marie in her wine-dark robes and ivory-colored veil, coming over to greet us with calm, rapid strides. She did not smile. Yet her grey eyes and patrician Irish face were serene and confident as she gathered us into her arms. Then, kneeling down, Mother Philomene kissed my brow, placing her hands firmly upon my shoulders as she spoke. Her words were plain; her tone evaded nothing and they burnt with the brave, tranquil flame of her faith: "And now you are in God's hands."

The Assumption was already crowded with women and children, and while our mothers waited in hushed anxiety, we children uproariously trampled over the flower beds and the white pebbled lanes of the luxuriant convent gardens. We were fully aware of the situation in which we were trapped but it seemed merely to heighten our excitement, our furious refusal to behave and be quiet. We were in hiding and we knew it, and we also knew that we would soon be caught. And the delirious rampages of Hide and Seek were not part of an ordinary game, for by our hysterical screams and laughter we were expressing the suppressed, nerve-taut shock of our terrified, whispering parents.

The Imperial Japanese Army entered Manila the night of January second — less than a month since the outbreak of war. By morning the Japanese Rising Sun flew over the United States high commissioner's residence, over the Malacañang Presidential Palace and over Fort Santiago in the Walled City. It was a damp, dark day. The skies were freighted with smoke from the dying fires that ringed the city. And we children went racing over the convent grounds, climbing the walls to look out into the streets and see the Japanese. But there was no one in the streets. Shrill birds flittered in the acacia trees and from within the convent there was a loud "school's out" of children's shouts. Otherwise, Manila seemed silent, motionless, deserted. Thousands fearing rape and famine had evacuated to the countryside; those who had stayed behind hid quietly in their homes, waiting. In the Assumption, the nuns and our mothers kept calling us down from the walls with the watchword of the day, a saying passed from person to person through every quarter of the forsaken city: "Don't attract attention."

2.

January sixth. The sun had almost set: darkness was issuing out of the earth, invading the underbrush, stealing over the lanes, obscuring all but the shapes of buildings and trees. We had been alerted by the sound of motors and were watching from behind the upstairs windows. And now there was a commotion at the convent gates and, as the gatekeeper opened them, three or four dilapidated cattle vans rattled in, grinding up the pebbled driveway and lunging to a halt before the convent buildings.

A Japanese soldier jumped out of the first truck and, catching sight of us peeping from the windows, shouted up, "All people! Every-body! One-two-three. Out-out — quick!"

The lamps at the convent doors went on. Led by the Reverend Mother, a delegation of nuns in deep burgundy robes walked in slow, formal procession out to meet the Japanese. Soldiers leapt from the cattle vans, small, quick men in khaki brandishing rifles with fixed bayonets. Stabs of Japanese shouts. Then the rich, Belgian voice of the Reverend Mother rose: "There are only women and their babies here."

My mother called me away from the window. The Japanese ordered the nuns to tell us to pack enough food and clothing for three days and assemble downstairs in ten minutes. We scrambled things into suitcases, rolled up pillows in blankets. Children wailed; their mothers were flushed and panicky. Soon the Japanese soldiers were up in the halls of the dormitory, shouting, angry. "All people! Out-side! Every-body. All Bree-tish — Amer-can, out-out!" Then they hustled the women and children down the stairs, prodding us with their bayonets into the yard. "In-side! In-side!" Bayonets pointed to the cattle vans. We were herded towards the trucks. Impossible to climb up into them, they were so high. The Japanese heaved luggage into the vehicles as women lifted each other up, were knocked down by luggage and then tried to help others up after them. Babies and children were passed from women on the ground up to their mothers in the trucks. One woman who had lost her child was about to come down. A soldier stopped her at bayonet-point and she stood screaming the child's name. I was hoisted up — the van was already packed; my mother was still on the ground. Fear in her eyes. Our friend Mrs. Macleod reached out her hand and helped Mother up. We were together again. The lost child had meantime been found and was being handed up to his mother. "They can't get any more of us in here!"

The Japanese soldiers, hysterical and shouting, forced more people into the truck. We were crushed together — women, babies, suitcases, bedding. The van gave a sudden lurch; women screamed. Bumped, jostled, stepping on toes — and we were off in darkness to an unknown destination. Babies were crying. Children asked, "Where are we going?" Women bickered with each other. Mother Philomene's words repeated themselves in my mind. Ladies, unused to such indelicate conveyance (some had rarely been in a crowded bus) , fell against each other as they were thrown by the swerve of the truck. "Would you *mind* not pushing?" "Well, *really!*" Mother pressed me to her; two women had exchanged slaps and it looked as if a brawl would follow. A voice began: "Pack up your troubles," and in a second a full chorus sang, "in your old kit bag," we children singing loudest of all, "And smile, smile, smile." Any song once started was swiftly joined by the lot of us. "My bonnie lies over the sea" — the van gave an abrupt wrench and a downward plunge, knocking us all over each other. "Bring back, oh, bring back." Someone lifted me over the side panels as a lookout. "We're at the river." The soldiers, having ignored the crossing at Santa Cruz Bridge, had driven halfway into the Pasig River. "Have you ever seen a lassie?" All the other cattle vans were behind us now; the children inside them had heard our singing and they were singing too. "Go this way," and we jolted forwards, "And that way," then backwards, "A lassie go this way" as the Japanese tried to back out of the river. "Go this way and that." When at last we battered backwards and out of the water, everyone in all the vans sang, "Glory, glory, hallelujah!"

The moon was well up, clear and clean against the sky, and we were still singing when our van came to a brake-squealing stop. The Japanese ordered us out: we had arrived at the University of Santo Tomás in north Manila. Jittery, flustered and breathing hard, we clambered down and then helped others after us. I found myself in a square before a vast concrete building. The building loomed before me, a grey solid mass in the centre of which rose a tower with a cross. Several women bantered briskly about Shanghai-Occidental architecture, saying that if only you blocked out the tower and took the building in with a squint it would look like Buckingham Palace. Others, who were in no mood for repartee, went frantic trying to keep their children together while they rummaged about for their luggage. The square was swarming with all sorts of people who had just been arrested, and squads of Japanese soldiers straddled up and down shouting at them. One mother had looped her brood of six to one another with a long rope and led them about like a string of pups. A contingent of British men had recently been brought in and several women found their husbands among them. Defiant levity spread through the throng like a brush fire: we would be here for three days at the most; Santo Tomás was being used for a civilian registration centre, certainly not as a concentration camp; everyone agreed that the stumpy little Japs were really rather funny in their crumpled uniforms and besides they would never dare — no, no, it was ridiculous. An Englishman, wearing a sun helmet in the moonlight, had neglected to bring his luggage. Instead he came with two bottles of whisky, a siphon of soda and paper cups, which he passed round. Nor was anyone particularly perturbed when word got about that the British were being segregated from the Americans.

A Japanese officer, with glasses like goggles, his trousers bagging over military boots, pranced up to us. He gave his orders in brutal, barking shouts, and as he legged over to various women, he cuffed them into place. "Amer-can! This-way! Bree-tish — over-there!" A great sick, sinking feeling surged over me in waves: I would be taken from my mother. For a moment or two I stood watching her, then followed her, dazed. With our passports in hand Mother had gone over to the officer taking easy, natural steps and approaching him politely from the side. She tried to explain: "Little boy has British passport; Mother, American passport."

The officer promptly got the point. He grabbed me by the arm and sent me hurtling at the group on the left. "Bree-tish! Over-there!" Murmuring protests rustled between the groups. While a bearded Scot reached over and put me back on my feet, I saw my mother, emphatic this time, walk firmly up to the officer. "No, you do not understand. The boy is *my* son with *British* passport. My *husband* is American. I have *American* passport." The Japanese officer stopped short; the muscles of his face worked in a convulsion of hate. "You, Amer-can-zu?" his lips went shooting out and he spat on her. Then, as a jeering noise from his throat broke into a stiff laugh, the officer struck her, a coarse clout, full on the side of her face. "Amer-can — hah? Go-there!" A kick from his military boot knocked her off balance and she went tottering and fell hard on the ground. "Mama — !" I started towards her, but the Scotsman quickly caught me and covered my mouth. "Hush, lad. Not a word." The American women were helping Mother up; she stood hunched and stunned, holding her hand over her ear. "Filthy yellow coolie," sputtered a man next me.

The Scot's beard brushed my ear as he whispered, "Go back of us now, and when he's not looking, run over to your mother." He nudged me behind him and I soon found many hands guiding me along behind the British lines and closer to the American sector.

The Japanese officer announced that we were under Japanese "protective custody" and would be responsible for our own meals. No one laughed. He concluded his announcement as two soldiers with bayonets joined him; then he turned sharply off down the square. I ran over to my mother and tugged at her dress; she was still holding her hand over her ear. Everyone was in quandary. What were we to do now? Were we dismissed? I felt all swollen up, hot and choked. Yes, someone said, we had been dismissed. My eyes smarted and a throbbing tightness filled my chest. Mother held me closely to her. We must find a place for the night.

We wandered towards the Main Building and had reached the entrance when something that had stuck between my heart and throat jerked suddenly free. "He kicked you, Mummy! Kicked you and hit you!" Now in the salt torrents of my anguish and resentment I began to blurt confusedly, accusing my mother for having been struck, as though somehow it were her fault.

People kept rushing past us as Mother stroked my hair and begged me not to cry, trying to gentle me with her voice. I only cried the more. She grew impatient, imperious. What could a mere child know about the war? I was to stop crying at once. Did I remember Kobe and Nagasaki, where Japanese women with babies slung to their backs had coaled the ships? Years before I was born she had seen those women not only with babies on their backs but with boys of my age beside them. "And I stood on the gangway of the *Empress of Asia* and saw those boys taken away by soldiers. Oh, the little brats cried and their mothers cried too, but it was off to the army for those poor mites. They're grown men now — look at them — the very same soldiers we see tonight."

The Japanese were stamping about, yapping at a group of elderly men in the square. Mother's lecture had not convinced me. I did not want anyone to hit my mother — from Kobe or anywhere else. Passersby were knocking into us; hysteria sharpened their voices. So I dried my tears and blew my nose on my shirt tail. "Come along then. We can't stand here all night," Mother said, picking up our blankets. "We shall have to find a place to sleep."

Santo Tomás was a bedlam. Two thousand men, women and children had been herded into the university grounds in the past three days. They milled about in the Main Building, trying to find their way back to their quarters, eating out of tins, hailing friends, complaining, looking for lost luggage, explaining, searching for the lavatory. Red Cross agents and volunteers worked in the hubbub, struggling to create order among this chaos of people who quite suddenly had become prisoners of war.

Mother led me through the corridors blazing with naked light bulbs and up to the volunteers who were assigning the new arrivals to rooms. The Main Building was already packed full. Chairs and school desks were jammed up in piles along the halls; people had covered the classroom floors with pillows, sheets and blankets, barely a foot apart from each other. No one could believe what had happened. Some were peeved: "Who in the hell do these Japs think they are?" Others were distraught: "Oh my God, I can't find my wife!" A young woman accosted us, shaking a ukulele in Mother's face, demanding, "How do you get OUT of this place?"

Mother brushed the girl and the ukulele aside. We pushed past the stunned crowds in the passageways of the Main Building and went out towards the Annex behind it. A man stood retching in the dark. In the Annex, teeming with women and children, we had been assigned to the first room on the right, where the only space left for us was over a stinking drain. Years in the tropics had given Mother a terror of the scorpions, poisonous spiders and snakes that came up from open drains.

"Oh, but we can't possibly sleep next to that!"

"You'll 'ave worse than that to sleep next to if these Nips do wot they did in Nanking," a red-faced woman tartly informed her.

We spread our blankets and pillows over the drain. The room was filled with British mothers and babies. Presently, when the red-faced woman lit a cigarette, a very genteel ash-blond lady raised a protest: "My dear madam, no smoking, please! You shan't mind if I suggest that there are over fifty of us in here. And we don't want a fire now, do we?"

The smell from the drain was foul. Mother was still shaken by the clout from the Japanese officer — he had struck her sensitive ear. In her childhood her eardrum had burst from scarlet fever. It was aching now and she moaned softly from the pain. We lay there foolishly on the floor, all the lights glaring into our faces as women squabbled in the room, flocks of people scurried to and fro in the corridor calling to each other and faces popped in at the open doorway asking for someone. I nestled up close to my mother and pretended to be asleep while she sighed from her aching ear. Where was Father, I wondered. We had not seen him since New Year's Day.

The last words I heard that night came from some rabid Barbara Frietchie loudly bitching in the corridor:

"Wait! You just wait! When Gener'l MacArthur hears about *this!* He'll fly the good old Stars and Stripes over this joint in just *two weeks!*"

3.

Next morning I awoke from a sound sleep, not quite remembering where I was until by degrees I became conscious of the concrete floor beneath our blanket and the stench of the drain and then began scratching at my mosquito bites. Mother was already sitting up, brushing her long, dark hair. There was no need to dress; we had slept in our clothes.

In the room women were gabbling with each other, attending to their children's needs and exclaiming that they had never spent such a night in their lives. Suddenly one of the babies pierced through the racket with a scream — his mother had stuck him with a pin. The red-faced woman, who knew all about babies, moved into action. "Poor little lambkin, did his Mumsie hurt him? Here, give 'im to me. I'll do his nappies for you. I've reared eight of me own, I have." And the rest of baby's pins were fastened without further protest. Few, if any, of the other women knew how to tend their young. Such tasks as preparing a bottle or changing a wet baby had been the exclusive domain of the amah.

It was a considerable distance to the lavatory; when we found it, there was a long queue of people bickering over priority. The constipated majority ruled: those with diarrhea were obliged to wait their turn.

When Mother and I were walking down the Annex corridor, trying to find our way to the Main Building, I noticed a friendly old gentleman in a grey felt hat and flannel suit; his face and his step quickened as he approached. All at once his grey eyes struck me as very familiar: it was my father.

And now we were in his arms, so overjoyed at being together again that we kept wandering back and forth, up and down the Annex corridors, talking and talking, Mother holding on to his right hand and I his left. Even my mother had not recognized Father at first: he looked so old and ill and his face was half shadowed by his grey hat. It was a shock not to see Father in his tropic whites, which perhaps had always made him look younger. Now he was trembling slightly from an attack of asthma and a chill.

Telling us he knew where some sort of breakfast was being

served, Father led the way behind the Main Building to an improvised canteen at which another, much longer queue had formed. When at last we received a bowl of cracked wheat and a mug of coffee there was no place left at the tables, so we had to sit on the ground.

At breakfast Father told us how he was arrested by the Japanese and taken to Villamor Hall at the University of the Philippines. Here he had spent three days locked in a classroom with a large group of other elderly men; they slept on tops of tables or sat through the nights in chairs. No food had come in for the first two days; there was no toilet, he said, and by the time they were brought to Santo Tomás, the condition of the room was pitiful. Father had a pack of cards in his pocket and spent much of his time trying to divert one of the men with a game of casino. The man had gone mad; he kept sidling up to new arrivals, buttonholing them and, with a sly, furtive wink, saying, "You know something? We're all going to be shot."

Our breakfast over, we made our way over to the Main Gate and joined the internees massed before the high wrought-iron railing that enclosed the grounds of Santo Tomás University. The day was hot from that fierce tropic sun which first warms you to the bone, then stifles you. Under the smothering sun we pushed our way through the dense crowd. I was seized by the sudden discovery: we were prisoners and forbidden beyond the spearheads of those iron bars. And this fact was ruthlessly impressed upon me by the khaki squads of Japanese soldiers manning the fence.

Outside the bars stood another mass of people, Filipinos waiting to make contact with the inmates of our prison camp. Many of them were wives or servants of the internees and stood patiently, for hours sometimes, until they caught sight of their husbands or employers. Some of the Filipinos carried picket signs or placards with the names of those whom they wished to reach; others attached notes to the ends of long sticks and prodded their messages between the bars. And then a cool, playful breeze came teasing through that oppressive heat: I had made another discovery — the freedom of laughter. It played all about me, delicate and intermittent, but quite as real as the Japanese soldiers and the iron bars. For everybody, on both sides of the railing, was remarkably jolly; they laughed, made silly jokes, waved and called to each other despite the glum soldiers and the bars.

Smack in the centre of the Filipino crowd stood the tallest man of all and round his neck, like some incredible boa, curled a gigantic fish the size of a shark. The tall man with a black shock of hair slanting over his handsome Oriental eyes kept gazing intently straight through the bars as if they did not exist; then, catching sight of us, he instantly brightened up and called, "Prising! Prising!"

Around Looming's broad shoulders was one of the finest fish in the Philippine seas, the enormous lapu-lapu, named after the Filipino chieftain who killed Magellan in 1521. The crowds on both sides of the railing went gusty with laughter as Looming began to lift the great fish over the tall pointed spearheads. But my parents were most embarrassed: Really! What a most extraordinary thing for Looming to bring. Whatever would we do with such a fish? A man beside us dryly suggested that we might even eat it.

More laughter, a hurricane of laughter, burst forth, followed by thundering cheers when the huge lapu-lapu was clumsily hoisted over the Spanish spearheads and triumphantly flopped onto the ground inside.

Everyone wanted to see the lapu-lapu; presently several young men offered to help Father carry the monster off to the camp canteen. I started after them, then stopped and turned as I suddenly remembered Looming and darted back, struggling through the crowds back to the railing. "Looming — ! Looming — !" I yelled, climbing up the iron bars until I held my hands round the spearheads. Two Japanese guards, the sun bright on their bayonets, lunged towards me. The crowds on either side of me began backing away with uneasy murmurs, for now the wind of fear was up. And although I crawled down from the bars I kept my shouting up, calling louder and louder until I was hoarse: "Looming —! Thank you! Goodbye! Goodbye! Looming —!" I could still see his head high above the far edges of the crowd: "LOOMING —!" But he did not turn back; Looming had not heard.

4.

Not many days after we were interned in Santo Tomás I noticed that my mother was up to something. She went quietly about, having confidential little chats with her friends in the Red Cross and among the Internee Committee. Soon I discovered that permits were being issued by the Japanese to transfer the ill and aged to hospitals. Father, as I knew, was sixty-four; he suffered from cardiac asthma and broke into chills at the least drop in temperature. My mother meanwhile complained of trouble with her ear and "a touch of dengue." Within a week both my parents were removed to the Philippine General Hospital in the south end of Manila. I do not remember how they broached this news to me, though I know that it came as no surprise and that I accepted their departure silently, heart-heavy with growing resentment that never dissolved. I could not believe that both of them could be ill at the same time; I felt that they cared only about being with each other, that they had abandoned me. And the rancor within me was cold, heavy and hard.

I was left in the care of Mrs. Harrington, wife of the previous British consul in Manila, until I could be sent to the Children's Home. A lean, aristocratic lady, Elsie Harrington was in charge of our room in the Annex, a task which she performed without fuss, preserving at all times a faint, endearing trace of humor. She kept an eye on me without appearing to do so, saw that I took my meals at the Annex kitchen and that I was safely in bed by eight o'clock curfew after she had called the roll. Unlike my parents, Mrs. Harrington treated me as if I were older than I was and, as a result, I grew up considerably in that brief time.

Although I felt betrayed by my parents, being left in Santo Tomás had its compensations. After all, I was an eight-year-old yearning to live in an adult world and during my fortnight in Mrs. Harrington's care I came as close to that world as possible. The confines of Santo Tomás were in themselves a world to me — a whole new world peopled by over two thousand internees, all of them uprooted from their regular lives and caught in the same crisis. The turmoil of the times brought their thoughts and feelings to the surface; the barriers were down and many people were quite eager to air opinions, complain, predict the future and talk to any man, woman or child who would listen.

Of course there were things that I heard about and could not understand. The Moral Patrol, for example. Everyone grumbled about it. I did not know what the word "moral" meant; however, I gathered that the Moral Patrol had something to do with discipline. It was established by the Internee Committee to avoid placing disciplinary measures directly in the hands of the Japanese. Sometimes the Moral Patrol had to enforce ridiculous rules by order of the Japanese commandant: married couples were forbidden to hold hands; women were forbidden to wear shorts. My parents had often held hands but they disapproved of the sort of women who wore shorts — vulgar. Drunkenness was punished by confinement in the camp jail. My father always took his glass of Scotch but never got drunk. Yet I knew what drunkenness could mean — it meant three British tars, roaring songs, arms round each other's necks, staggering about on shore leave in Shanghai.

I listened to everything anyone said about the Japanese. They were generally regarded as an army of coolies, slit-eyed, bandy-legged, misbegotten little monsters of an inferior race — we had been captured by a tribe of malicious monkeys that had just leapt out of the trees. And I also learnt how the Japanese people originated: Once upon a time, many years ago, a shipload of Chinese had been wrecked on the coast of the Japanese isle of Honshu. The Chinese married monkeys (for there were no people in Japan) and the inevitable result was the army that had taken us prisoner. This story I did not believe, for I remembered the elegant Japanese ladies smiling at me from their sedan chairs at Kamakura. On the other hand I was tempted to believe the story when I came face to face with some of the Japanese guards. I'd had, after all, no previous experience of soldiers.

Occasionally there was speculation on a touchy subject, the bombing of Pearl Harbor. Was it a *surprise* attack?

"Whole thing was a hoax. Roosevelt knew it was coming. We knew it was coming. I bet he knew the day and the hour."

"Aw, come on. It was just bungling; plain American bungling."

"Nope. He wanted this war. Takes care of unemployment. But he had to let the Japs strike first so as he could shut them isolationists up back home."

"Hey, whatsa matter? Ain't you patriotic?"

"Quite impartially, I should say that in the long run you Americans have everything to win."

"What about all those guys that got killed? What about us?"

"They don't count. We don't count."

After the shock of the first weeks wore off, people in Santo Tomás began to settle down for a brief but indefinite period. The Filipino-American forces were hanging on at Bataan and Corregidor and, despite the occupation of Manila, the Americans still blocked Japanese access to Manila Bay. Soon Roosevelt's promised reinforcements would arrive: it was merely a question of two or three months before we were set free. Meantime, some of the wealthier pessimists had built makeshift bamboo huts within the university grounds, where they whiled away the time in secret games of poker and bridge.

We were no longer allowed to stand at the railing near the gate and look for our friends through the bars. It was undignified, the Japanese declared, for those in their custody to be fed through the bars, like animals in the zoo. Food, beds, mattresses, cooking pots and laundry were received from the package line that formed every morning and afternoon. Everything that came into the camp was inspected (though not very thoroughly) by the Japanese guards. At certain hours Filipino pedlars were permitted to hawk their wares, and those of us who had money could purchase shoestrings, fruit, writing paper and Filipino sweets. Mrs. Harrington had been left with cash for my allowance, which she carefully doled out every day and which I spent on delicious coconut-rice cakes.

For a week I had my little bag packed with my toothbrush, clothes and dominoes, ready to leave for the Children's Home. It was not easy to get permission for me to go to the Home because the Japanese, at that time, decreed only children under seven eligible. Twice I had assembled with a group of younger children in the plaza before the Main Building and twice I was told that the request for my transfer had been denied. And each time I was secretly glad. I did not want to be sent to the Children's Home. I wanted to remain in Santo Tomás where my parents had left me and where I expected them to return from hospital. Also, I had rarely been with other children and should far sooner have been caged with wild cheetahs in a zoo. The last time I was told to report in front of the Main Building I had been tempted to hide, but such behavior seemed too childish, too contrary to my adult pretentions; so, with an effort, I got a grip on myself and let Mrs. Harrington take me to the group of mothers and children in the plaza. When the car arrived, I was the first to enter it; the other children began crying as their mothers put them in with me. Then the mothers stood outside the car and sang:

> Wish me luck
> As you wave me
> Goodbye.
> Cheerio
> Here we go
> On our way.

The words and tune of that song still twist my heart as they did that day long ago. I can still feel the car start smoothly as I hold a hard stone inside me, guts stiffening with fear, my throat big as a goiter where my tears are choked back. And now, while we are whisked off by strangers to some place *unknown,* I can see all the mock smiles and waving hands which go with that trite, plucky song.

Jewels of the Virgin

THE CHILDREN'S HOME was established by a young Filipina child-specialist, Doctor Fé del Mundo. Charming and practical as her name suggests, she had talked the Japanese authorities round until they gave her permission to establish a refuge for children. I was particularly fascinated by a great bottle with a still-born infant that was displayed on her office bookcase.

In this large Spanish house there were some fifteen children put two or three to a room. Everything was spotlessly white: white iron bedsteads, white blankets, white mosquito nets and white painted walls. At night, some of the children woke up crying and well-starched Filipina nurses hurried to their bed-sides with thermometers. The symptoms were often the same: homesickness, they called it.

One afternoon, during the siesta, a nurse sent me downstairs to the *sala* — someone had come to visit me. Who could it be? Looming, perhaps? Terray? Or Alfredo? I hastened down the stairs and flung open the parlor door. Joy first, then a flush of embarrassment. Dressed in pyjamas, slippers and a hospital robe, my father stood in the centre of the room. I was about to jump into his wide-open arms when I suddenly stopped short — a Japanese guard waited behind him holding a rifle. Through the window I could see the horse and carriage that brought them. Father looked stripped of everything, even of self-respect.

For a moment I stood there unable to move or speak, wavering between humiliation and pity at seeing my father in his pyjamas, a prisoner watched by a guard. I wished he had not come, then went hot with guilt and shame. My feelings must have shown plainly in my face, yet Father came over to me, his grey, brown-flecked eyes smiling only with reassurance.

He had come, he told me, from Philippine General Hospital where he was in the war prisoners' ward and Mother was in another ward upstairs with the women. Then Father explained that the Children's Home would soon be changing quarters, and that he was given a special pass to visit me before we left. The Japanese soldier glanced at his watch. Father asked me to be a good, brave boy. Would I give him my word, honor bright? I had barely stammered my promise when the soldier tapped at his watch. Our ten-minute visit was up. My papa kissed me and gave me a big hug that smelt strongly of hospital. And as he went out with his guard, I remained in the sala, my sobs wrestling within me. I must not let the other children see me cry. From the shady whiteness of the room I stared through the white window curtains and could see my father climbing into the carromata, followed by his Japanese guard. With a flick of the *cochero*'s whip on the horse, the carriage started off down the white, hot street.

The Children's Home was now permitted to take children up to the age of twelve. We were told that we were leaving for larger quarters in a wing of the Holy Ghost Convent. With our clothes packed into little bundles, we sat waiting in the sala for the cars to come and take us away. Two very young Japanese soldiers waited with us; they seemed quite green and fresh from their homes. When several smaller children began crying, the soldiers gulped and looked painfully embarrassed. They stretched out their hands to us and tried to make friends, but they were enemy soldiers and we shook our heads. Afterwards, when the soldiers accompanied us to the cars, one of them dropped his rifle and we giggled at him. As he stooped to pick it up, he glanced over at us and frowned, shamed by his clumsiness and the laughter of children — then he gave us a bashful, boyish grin.

2.

War rumors and war news always got round to the new Children's Home. True or false, they came in with the busload of parents on their fortnightly visits or arrived with the mistresses from the camp — few of the mistresses ever remained more than a month or two. The boots of the Imperial Japanese Army trampled over South-East Asia, and at each victory the occupation troops in Manila celebrated with triumphal marches. Despite the onslaught of Japanese, the Filipino-American forces on Bataan and Corregidor held out grimly against them, awaiting the reinforcements that would never come. Day and night, when the wind came in from the west, we could hear the guns of Corregidor.

3.

I was put in a dormitory with thirty other young boys — caged with worse than cheetahs, quite as I expected. Two rows of beds flanked either side of a passageway; at the foot of each bed was an old-fashioned school desk and chair. Above the blackboard at the head of the room hung a huge crucifix that seemed to hover over us.

Sweeney Gimp was the ringleader. The other boys adored Sweeney; he was chief chick of our roost and they would do anything for him. He had green eyes with dark lashes and curly, drab-blond hair. The boys thought Sweeney the handsomest among them. I disagreed — his nose was freckled and snub.

Sweeney had it in for me; I could tell by the look in his green eyes. I knew he had something up his sleeve, though I did not guess that it was a trump card he was keeping for a birthday greeting. When my ninth birthday came along, the mistresses made a fuss about it and the boys all had to sing "Happy Birthday." Sweeney sang too, his malicious smirk emphasizing the snub of his nose. He looked decidedly pretty as he sang — pretty and nasty.

That evening after lights-out, the boys begged and coaxed at Sweeney to tell them a story, as he often did. It was the usual one — about his mother's death.

"She wuz lyin' in her coffin. She wuz smilin' and her hand reached right out and took a-hold of mine."

"Honest, Sweeney? Gee! Oooooh, Sweeney!"

"Prising hasn't got a mother," he announced that night, playing his trump. "He's a little bastard."

"I do have a mother." I had never heard such nonsense.

"Not a *real* mother. You're adopted. That means your real mother hated you so much that she didn't wanna keep you."

Bastard! I had heard that word before: "bastard brat" my mother had called me when I pricked Fräulein Winkel with the badge. *Adopted?* Yes, I had seen that word — it was in my British passport: "The bearer is the adopted child of Mr. and Mrs. Frederic William Prising, both American citizens, from whom he assumed the surname Prising." I had never paid it any attention before.

Sweeney's little birthday present had truly pierced my Achilles' heel and, though I tried not to show it, I limped long afterwards. I did not have *real* parents — that was why Mother and Father had left me to go into hospital together. That too was why the other children's parents came to visit them twice a month. Then I thought of Father's visit, of how I had wished that he had not come, and I felt even worse. I began to brood. What *did* "bastard" mean? I must ask my British friends, Derek and Chris Bure.

"Heaps of great men were bastards," Derek assured me. "It

only means your real parents weren't married," Chris said. "I say, how do you think Sweeney found out?" I told them about my passport, which I kept locked in my luggage. "Not very likely," Derek continued. "Somebody must have told him." "There we are!" Chris's brain always worked with his brother's. "He'd have got it from someone who knows your people." In no time whatever we tracked the chatterbox down: one of the mistresses, a friend of my mother's, who had given the information to Sweeney. Now she was confronted by a nine-year-old, demanding that she, a grown woman, repeat her gossip. With the help of a few adroit questions from Derek and Chris, we learnt that I was indeed adopted and that the story had been published in the Manila press.

4.

"They're here — ! They've come back — the Americans!" Sweeney howled in the dead of night. I woke; the whole building was shaking and rocking. "Air raid! Wake up! Air raid!" I yelled, jumping out of bed and dropping flat on my belly to the floor. The building shuddered while the cries of awakening children rose up like wild birds in the jungle. Nuns and mistresses came hurrying into the dormitory: "It's an earthquake." The tremors persisted; they grew less violent; then it was over.

That was our last mistake: until that night every slam of a door or sudden thunderclap had been taken for the return of the American forces. But the earthquake was indeed a portent, for the next day came the first reports of the defeat of Bataan. Everybody refused to believe them, just as they refused to believe that General MacArthur had escaped to Australia. Japanese propaganda! Who but a fool could believe that the Japanese could defeat the American and Filipino armies?

Slowly, in broken fragments, stories of the Death March were smuggled into the Children's Home.

We're the battling bastards of Bataan
No mama, no papa, no Uncle Sam . . .

Thousands upon thousands of Filipino and American troops marched from Bataan to San Fernando, in many different groups, shell-shocked and exhausted. They drank the water from ditches and died of dysentery; they died of malaria. Some marched asleep; others stumped on as they clung to the shoulders of men who still had two legs. They walked in the blistering sun, a defeated army, prodded by pitiless victors. When the wounded and sick straggled and dropped by the wayside, they were run through with bayonets; they were shot; or they were blindfolded and had their heads hacked from their bodies by Japanese sabres. Blood spurting everywhere, the headless men would fall forwards, their slowing heartbeats still pumping blood in spouts, bright red at first in the sunlight until it darkened and was absorbed into the parched earth. The bands of survivors continued their marches, many to die at San Fernando, others to die in the military prison camp at Cabanatuan. Today the Death March, like Hiroshima and Nagasaki, has become part of history. For a few it is still a memory; for the rest, merely another fact of the Second World War.

5.

After the fall of Bataan and Corregidor, the Japanese issued temporary releases for the ill, the elderly and mothers with children to live in their Manila homes. Although the other boys' parents spent an entire Sunday with them every fortnight, I had not seen mine in over five months. But about this time I did have a surprise visit from Terray. She told me that my father and mother were no longer in hospital but living in our flat in the Spanish lady's house. Now that I knew they were safely home and had not sent for me, my dormant rancor woke; it had grown in its sleep and become stronger and bolder than when I was left behind in Santo Tomás.

Alien to most of the boys at the Children's Home, I began to retreat into myself, building castles in the air, daydreaming of life after the war. Stopped only by the ringing Angelus, when I knelt and prayed, I went far from the boys at play, wandering towards the private reaches of the convent grounds. Out from the sun-blazing garden of the Children's Home, I strayed into the shaded convent close, past a pond of water lilies, and beyond it to a bridge of black, crumbling stone that led up to the grotto grown round with ferns and decorated with shells. It was a replica of the spot in Lourdes where Bernadette Soubirous had had visions of the Holy Virgin. Dappled by sunlight, the entire setting was magical and beautiful — except the statue of the Virgin itself, which was the usual cold, plaster figure in white robes and turquoise sash, with a simpering face and one foot stepping upon a serpent, the symbol of evil.

Often, towards late afternoon, I found myself returning to the secluded shrine, mesmerized by a gold paper crown bedizened with glass jewels that the nuns had made and placed upon the statue's head. It reminded me of the crowns I helped my mother make for her plays. And gazing at the statue, I prayed to the Virgin Mary (whom the nuns said was mother of us all) and asked to be sent home to my parents. A faint cloud began to grow over the plaster figure until the statue came gradually to life. At the same time I knew that what was happening was a fantasy, a vision, but it was real all the same. Her lips moved; she was murmuring words that I could not distinctly hear except as I heard the voice of the sea when I held a mollusc shell to my ear. The cloud round the statue grew shimmering-bright and it became Kwannon, goddess of mercy and motherhood, as well as Mary the Virgin. Only the crown had not changed: it was made of gold paper and paste jewels; it sat false upon her head. But the seashell voice came clearly now: "The jewels . . . I give you the jewels . . ." Slowly I reached up and one by one I plucked the jewels from the crown, then put them in my pocket.

As I did so, the vision vanished and only a simpering plaster statue remained.

When the jewels were discovered missing, the scandal broke. A sacrilege had been committed within the sacred grounds! The Virgin's shrine was desecrated! When, by the fifth day, the scandal had reached its height and Sister Sanctissima, Sister Redeemer, the mistresses and the children had formed search parties, I broke my silence. "Sweeney," I whispered, catching the beam from his bright green eye, "want to have a look?" And I reached down into my pocket and showed him the handful of glass jewels. I knew that I need do nothing more; he would do the rest.

Sister Sanctissima sent me to the chapel where I knelt on the hard floor through the dull afternoon, repeating the rosary, pinching the black beads between my fingers and crawling on my knees as Spanish penitents do.

Late that evening, as I was being sent up to bed, Sister Redeemer unknowingly became the instrument of the Holy Virgin. But the nun was an imperfect medium and her words came harsh — though they were miraculously transformed in my ears: "We can't have a thief staying here. Your parents are living at home — you can go back to them."

Under House Arrest

DOÑA CONCEPCIÓN AGUILAR, who had let the top floor of her house to us, was *una pobre viuda* — an unfortunate widow. Under her red, swollen ferret's eyes her puffy cheeks were netted by the lines of age. The old lady was said to have come of very good family, which perhaps accounted for her perpetual headaches, her *migranos*. Since she lived on reduced means, she kept no servants, unless her niece, Rosario, could be considered a servant. While Doña Concepción sat in a straight-backed chair and complained of her headaches, Rosario did the old lady's marketing, her washing, her ironing and even her cooking, and also tended the wartime vegetable garden. Early in the morning, during siesta or in the hollows of the night, we heard Doña Concepción's voice creaking like a door on a rusty hinge — "Rosario! Rosario!" — as if summoning the girl to her deathbed. Everyone loved Rosario for her innocent smile and cheerful ways. We knew that she would never marry nor ever be rich. Indeed, when her ugly old aunt died, the reduced means would undoubtedly be left to say masses for the repose of Doña Concepción's soul and then Rosario would become a nun.

When I arrived home my reception had been fairly cool: I was uncertain, at first, whether I was being punished for a jewel thief or whether my parents merely considered me an annoyance. In any case, Sally welcomed me eagerly with barks, jumps and wags of her stump of a tail, and when I was sent to my room she spent the afternoon gazing up at me in grateful resignation as I picked out hundreds of ticks from her spaniel ears.

By suppertime I gradually realized that my parents had greeted me as if I had returned from some casual errand down the street. Evidently they were pretending that nothing in the past six months had really happened; that our life was a continuation of the days when Manila was declared an open city, before we sought refuge in the Assumption, before we became prisoners of war. When I sat with my parents as the shadows dulled the dusk-pink light on the verandah, I shattered their evasions by asking about my adoption.

Father burst into a fit of coughing and spluttered, "What kind of a question is that?" And Mother started slightly, murmured "Adopted?" and, rising gracefully, slipped over to a different chair. "Whoever told you that? No, you were *chosen*." The rose-grey shadows lengthened as she smoothed the folds of her dress. "Ask me no more of your foolish questions. Bastard, my eye! You've been paying attention to a silly lot of bad boys."

Napoleon was dead. His empty cage stood in the window of the sitting room, which was bare of any furniture. Well, he was *gone* anyway. I was told that Napoleon had taken a severe chill and was presently helping the tomatoes to grow in the kitchen garden.

Terray, with her five-month-old baby and her sister, came to visit us the day after I arrived. How disgracefully I had been tying my shoes at the Children's Home! "Never mind, Terray. Let him tie them as he will. All's upside down in these times." Mother's little spit curls at her ears had gone quite grey; her eyes had a haunted look which they would never lose. Terray's sister sprayed herself liberally with scent; then she sprayed the baby playing on the floor and then me. Terray was fretting about her husband, who had joined the troops at Bataan in Christmas week. "Oh mum, every day I pray in the church," she was saying as Mother led her out of my room. "I do not know if he is still alive. But God maybe is angry because Julio is dead and I do not wear a black dress." Her sister sang the baby a dirty song about a girl with a backside like a *bulaklak,* which means "flower" in Tagalog. I could hear Mother's voice drifting from a further distance: "I shall pray for your Julio too and the good Lord will surely grant our prayers . . ." Terray's crying mingled with Mother's fading words of comfort. The sister had picked up the baby and was rocking it in her arms. "No more papa, maybe," she said with a shrug. Then she produced the scent again and added confidingly, "Aqua Velva — expensive American. Better than no-good Jap stuff, smell like shit."

The wet season came, turning the skies a doomsday dark; they glowered and threatened, then thrashed the city with rain. Puddles accumulated in the garden, the dust in the lanes turned into mud and mosquitoes began to breed. Father wheezed from his asthma; he fretted and fumed, then sadly shook his head and reclined in his sloping planter's chair. What had he brought his wife to? While he put me through my lessons or reread his Rudyard Kipling, Mother was slaving away in the kitchen. And he could not forgive himself. He had been a millionaire when they married; a decade later he had lost his fortune. Now he was growing old. He was trapped in an occupied city, an enemy alien, and forbidden to earn his living, while his wife had become his cook!

What Father did not know is that Mother thrived on these unfamiliar tasks. Old menus that Alfredo had followed for years were quite useless — they required imported ingredients — but Mother loved inventing new recipes. She played the martyr with pleasure and enjoyed wringing her hands as she arrived faint and sweating from the kitchen. But she would have loathed it if Father had not fretted and fumed.

2.

We rarely had visitors. But we had already seen him from the verandah when he jangled the bell at the garden gate. From beneath us we could hear Doña Concepción's deathly croak: "Rosario! Pronto, pronto, niña. Un soldado. Ay-ay-ay! Mi cabeza! qué dolor — qué migrano!" Then the chimes of Rosario's voice: "Sí, tía, momento. Paciencia." We watched Rosario going out past her vegetable garden with the afternoon sun playing on her brown, curly hair.

Father sent me to my room. On my way, I found Alfredo peering from behind the Coromandel screen in the dining room. "Go quick to the broom closet in the kitchen and hide," he told me. I preferred the broom closet: a spy might hide in a broom closet but only children were sent to their rooms. The Japanese officer came up the steps, his samurai sword rattling its chains, tapping the tiles. Then I could hear voices, though not what they said. I slipped from the broom closet and into the hallway.

"Psst! Alfredo! Psst!"

"Go back to the broom closet," Alfredo whispered, remaining at his post.

Presently I heard my mother's voice with its silvery rise and fall, each word distinct, and behind her tone all the studied ease of an actress on an opening night.

"Oh yes — my dear Colonel. I have indeed been to Japan. Many, many times. Such a beautiful country you have — Nikko, Miyanoshita, Nara. Do you by chance know my dear friend Madame Yamaguchi? Her husband was for some time your consul at Harbin."

The little brass bell for Alfredo tinkled. Leaving his sentinel post behind the Coromandel screen, he went on bare, silent feet to the verandah. Mother's voice lowered in a naturalistic manner, giving orders to Alfredo. In a moment he was back, white with fury and shaking all over, as he hustled about the kitchen.

"He is sitting down. Mum wants tea. She said you will go out to them now."

The Japanese officer sat on the verandah chatting quite amicably. Father assumed an air of polite interest, nodding his head every so often. In the centre chair, Mother presided, emitting perfectly timed little sighs of pleasure and of sympathy. Absolutely dumbfounded, I took my seat in the furthest rattan chair.

The Japanese officer was saying, "I have come because I am so lonely man. Wife, babies — all in Japan." He drew several snapshots out from his pocket. "Three babies I have, see?"

Mother took the pictures in her best theatre fashion (drawing-room comedy, 1911: *Lady Mannerly's Colonel*), holding them in her left hand, lower and at a greater distance than one would in real life — unless one were far-sighted — so that the gesture "carried." Her right hand, meanwhile, described light rapid gestures of delight while her voice, suiting the word to the action, glided over her lines, sacrificing neither style nor spontaneity.

"My dear, what pretty ones!" And with dulcet, rippling laughter, "Aha! This I can see is the clever one, yes?" She showed it to the officer, and when he beamed his assent, she added, "Oh, and this little boy will always love his mother." She tossed the line away, so that she could enrich the next with high sentiment, the voice lowering as if she must restrain an impulse to weep. "But the *baby* — the baby loves only you, my dear Colonel, all for her very own."

Suitably impressed, the Japanese officer rubbed his hands enthusiastically. He blushed and giggled. "Yes. Yes. Yes. Baby-girl she loves the father best."

Alfredo entered with the tea tray. Mother poured out a flashing stream of tea into a cup and handed it to Alfredo.

"Tea, Colonel? We love our tea just as you do in Japan. No biscuits, alas. I'm afraid your army has taken them all away."

I felt sure that Mother had gone too far this time. There was a pause as Alfredo passed the cup to the Japanese. It continued while Mother poured tea for Father, for herself and for me. She broke the pause.

"You may go, Alfredo."

Mother sipped tea, Alfredo left on cue and Father sat comfortably as ever in his planter's chair. I glanced anxiously at the officer; perhaps he had not understood. Smiling agreeably, Mother stirred her tea: the play was going well; she could afford the extended pause. She merely sat looking at her Colonel, expectantly awaiting his reply.

"War is very bad," he began softly. "Many things we have no more. Forgive if my English is — much broken, slow. I want very much talk in English." His face, naive and friendly, became grave. "After war — after war is over. Everybody speak English. Understand?"

"Really, my dear Colonel? I believe everyone should speak many languages. I should speak yours and you mine." Again her voice lowered with restrained emotion. "But you, dear Colonel, speak English so well. I cannot talk in your language — I know such a few, very few words of Nipponese."

When the officer had finished his cup of tea, he bowed ceremoniously, thanked us and then descended the verandah steps, his sword just touching the yellow tiles as he went.

"By Jove!" Father exclaimed, "you certainly knew how to talk to him. Only thing I could do was to mention the weather. Gosh, beloved, I'll wager you'd have kept the League of Nations together."

That was not the only call Mother's Japanese colonel paid. He arrived several times, so Mother played benefit matinees. Whenever the bell rang at the garden gate, Doña Concepción would groan for Rosario and up the Japanese officer came. He brought us biscuits and gave Father cigars. Mother showed him the statue of Kwannon and once, when he expressed interest in

Shakespeare, Mother cast drawing-room comedy aside and, beginning simply, rising gradually to a full, but well-modulated climax, she recited Portia's mercy speech.

On his final visit we had no proper tea, so the officer drank ginger-root tea instead. As he bade us farewell, he mentioned he was going to leave and would see his wife and three children. They lived, he told us, in Nagasaki.

I asked Mother why he came. To check up on us? To practice his English because he knew Japan would lose the war? Or was he really lonely? Mother thought awhile and said, "Possibly a bit of all three."

3.

We were confined to the house except for brief trips to churches or hospitals within the Malaté district. And if we ventured into the streets, we were obliged to wear the bright red armbands that branded us as enemies of Japan.

"Alfredo simply can't find the food we need at market," Mother was saying as she stepped from her room, "so we shall have to go shopping ourselves."

The transformation was incredible, her costume perfect. Indeed, Mother might have been the sister of Doña Concepción Aguilar in the worn black dress and black stockings, her hair piled high and fastened with a great tortoiseshell comb borrowed from Rosario. Mother had dusted her face with rice flour, which lent her the appearance, both pallid and meagre, so typical of genteel Spanish poverty.

"Laugh if you will," she said, giving me a peremptory glance, "but we'll be safer as Spaniards than wearing stupid red armbands. Come along, then. Put on your *camisa* and we're off to market."

We walked down our street under the pressure of a humid afternoon, apprehensive lest we be noticed by neighbors: the pro-Japanese Rameras in particular, who kept their eye on us.

As we passed their house I tried to step as softly as my wooden clogs would let me. No one was stirring for it was still in the siesta hour but we were well up San Andrés and had turned into Calle Marcellino before we felt easier. Mother had thrust a musty black veil over her shoulders and she carried a market bag made of matting; we spoke in low murmurs as we stepped along the cracked pavements, looking neither left nor right. I led the way, avoiding the occasional Japanese sentry posts, taking the smaller byways until we reached the marketplace at Paco.

At once the crowded market with its activity and din lifted our spirits. Fish, fruit and flies, it was familiar old Manila, much good-humored haggling and banter in Tagalog, absolutely Filipino. Its lively anarchy defied the oppression of the conquered city.

"Mira, Mama — mangos, qué bonitos!" But the mangos were too expensive, the avocados badly bruised and small. So Mother in her dainty Castilian lisp began bargaining for calamansis. The fruit vendor, whose eyes made cruel slits, refused to bring down the price. He spoke little Spanish and his lips curled as he asked Mother, sharply, "Habla inglés?" "Poco, poco," she replied softly. "Three pesos is too much." The vendor said, "Bad times. Everything is very dear."

"Yes, I know." Mother's tone had changed; she looked the vendor straight in the eye, making no further attempt in Spanish, and spoke with a curious combination of pride, humility and strength: "And these times have made us poor. We cannot pay high prices." The fruit vendor's expression gradually shifted: "Ah, English? You are English? American?" She went cold. But the vendor became suddenly excited, anxious. He grabbed as many calamansis as his hands could hold and rushed over to her. "Here, please — I don't sell to you, please — you take." Mother choked on his kindness; she trembled; she could scarcely speak. "No, no — I must pay you — here," she said, fumbling in her purse, then pressing some money into his hands.

The legion of flies that buzzed the marketplace seemed to pass

from stall to stall, like messengers bearing the word of our arrival. Prices began to drop; faces behind the stalls greeted us
with broad smiles and conspiratorial winks; shoppers nodded to
us as if we were old friends. The vegetable man produced
onions, which were costly and rare, from his secret sack — two for
the price of one. Our fruit vendor came hurriedly back to us
with a big papaya: "Please — my present to you. I am Narciso.
You tell if your houseboy comes that Narciso will make a good
price."

An abrupt change ran through the marketplace. Faces of stall
keepers closed. Loud voices came from a short distance away.
Shouts. We were just in front of an ancient fishmonger, gold
hoops in her ears, her teeth blood-red from chewing betel nut,
cracked, parched skin stretched over the bones of her face.
Quickly she sprang at Mother, pushed her behind the stall and
forced her roughly to the ground, placing a round woven tray
heaped high with tiny stinking fish in Mother's lap. "Japs come!
Japs come!" cried the old fishmonger as she took off her black
shawl and threw it over Mother's head, hiding all but her chin.
"Robin, turn your back," Mother commanded. Whispers
rushed about us. "Kempe Tai! Military police!" I knew what
that meant — the Japanese Gestapo.

Japanese voices fired directly behind me. "Amer-can? Bree-
tish? Where? Where is the enemy aliens?" The Filipino faces
before me were poker faces. The voices of the military police
shot again: "Where go the Amer-can?" I heard a scuffle, then
a woman crying. She must have been slapped. A man, big-
bellied as a Chinese Buddha, gave a great stretch and yawn;
another man made ambiguous gestures and glanced with liquid
eyes towards heaven. The whistling fishmonger's boy settled
casually on his haunches. "Over there!" said a Filipina woman
behind me. "See — over there!" We were caught. It was only a
matter of seconds before the Kempe Tai took us. Christ, how I
wanted to turn round, to meet them face to face. But I stood

rigidly with my back to them, trying to stop my knees from quivering as I stared at my mother. Her head was bent low over the platter of stinking fish; a black cloud of flies hovered in front of her, alighting on the shawl, circling above the silvery fish. "Here they are — go that way! Quick! Catch them!" This Filipino voice, however, was not so close as the last. And then, from distance further off, the military police went into a terrible fit of angry shouts. Stamping, the sound of things crashing, tables knocked down. "Over here! Over here!" shrilled a woman's voice from the outer margin of the marketplace. Instantly the voices of all the vendors in the distance took up the cry: "Look — they are here!" "Quick, catch them!" "They go there!"

The faces of the Filipinos in front of me began to soften, their eyes unshuttered and brightened in triumph. An old man broke into a toothless grin of gums. "Japs all go the wrong way!" He began to laugh. Presently laughter rang and shook through the marketplace, scattering the droves of flies high into the sunlight.

Narciso came running back to us. "Come along, mum, quick! The Japs will come back." The old fishmonger had set the tray of fish aside and was helping Mother up as she removed the shawl. And then Mother and the wizened old woman were hugging fast to each other, crying.

"Oh no, mum, no! Time to go!" Narciso exploded, pulling the two part, catching me by the hand, then hustling us towards the opposite side of the market. He was crying now. The three of us wept — Mother, Narciso and I — not from panic but overwhelmed by love. As we ran through that marketplace of unknown friends, we were all stripped to the human essentials and the feelings we shared were vast and wonderful. Over two hundred persons in the Paco market, any one of whom might have been shot, had protected a woman and child. We hastened past smiling faces, past heads held high, past hard-worn hands with crooked fingers raised in the V for Victory, past humble hands that made the sign of the cross as we passed. Vendors stuffed

Mother's market bag to bursting with vegetables and rice. In the chaos of those times we were all one, sharing the tragedy and strife of war, and what had become important was not nationality or language, not patriotism or race or class, but rather that we were all civilians oppressed by an army. Human life was essential and what we wanted was the true freedom, not the slogans of governments for which men fight, but the freedom to live our individual lives in peace.

Narciso led us out into the ringing brightness of the sun and smuggled us into a horse cart where we hid behind hanging rows of bananas. The young, round-faced cochero smirked agreeably as he raised his whip to the horse: "Where you want to go, crazy-folk?"

"Malaté — between San Andrés and Cortabitarté."

When the carretela reached our garden gate, the cochero pulled us out from behind the bananas and gave us the ripest ones; then he, who would always be poor, refused our money.

Father greeted us on the verandah. Still shaking from the excitement, we had scarcely begun our story when Rosario came running up the steps. "Santa Maria! Oh, thank God you are back. Today, this afternoon, the Kempe Tai arrested hundreds of people — in the Escolta, at shops and in the markets — anybody who wore the red armband. All are taken to Fort Santiago."

But we did not escape for long. Soon after my tenth birthday (when Mother Philomene told me, "You are two numbers now. Quite grown-up — you will never be more than two") a questionnaire arrived:

> Where do you get money to live on?
> Are Filipinos helping you?
> Who is helping you?

We answered the questions with lies. We said that we lived by selling personal effects. Alfredo had indeed sold our silver to a Syrian merchant but the money was consumed in three months by galloping inflation. Prisoners of war both in Santo Tomás and under temporary release lived on the charity of Filipinos, of the Swiss, Chinese, Spaniards, even Germans who risked their lives by lending or giving us money. My father's friends dared not visit us but sent their servants to meet Alfredo at the Malaté Church where the business was performed by aid of the three Irish priests, Father Hinehan, Father Lawlor and Father Kelly, in the secrecy of the confessional. Many who helped civilian prisoners of war died of wounds at Fort Santiago or were shot by the Kempe Tai without trial; some simply disappeared or were killed in the Battle for Manila. I never knew the names of our friends, or the stories of their individual deaths.

In April 1943, my parents were ordered to return to the Philippine General Hospital and I was to be detained in the Jesuit college, Ateneo de Manila, now a detention centre for women and children. Not long before, reports reached us of an Allied offensive in South-East Asia, although for over a year afterwards it was rumored that the American forces would take Formosa as a steppingstone to Japan and the Philippines would be passed by.

Sally was put to sleep; no one could afford to feed her. Mother's pet Persian, Smoky Moonlight, fared better since the rat population had increased and she was given away as a ratter. After I left for the Ateneo, our last home was disbanded; what valuables remained were stored either with Rosario or the Irish priests at the Malaté Church. Nothing would be spared from the looting, the fires and the eventual massacre in the Battle for Manila. But of Sally's death and the breakup of our home I merely guessed or learned much later, for then I was a child, and children are never told.

Children's Games

MY INTERNMENT at the Ateneo proved to be a stroke of good luck: the back of the Philippine General Hospital overlooked our enclosed courtyard, thus making it possible for me to slip over to see my parents every afternoon. During my visiting hour, the Japanese guard was usually absent from his post, though he turned up twice to receive his bribe — a roll of "Mickey Mouse" money — from the Irish priest who smuggled me through the wire fence. Once I had got through the fence and into the hospital, the Filipino doctors and nurses hustled me to the men's internment ward. Papa would be waiting at the door; he would greet me with a great hug and then proudly take me to meet his cronies.

The grand old-stager of the ward, Mr. McCulloch-Dick, had been given up for dead when he was brought into hospital. He was the founder and publisher of the Philippines *Free Press*, which before the war sharply criticized Japanese militarism and Japan's alliance with Nazi and Fascist powers. After the fall of Manila, he was arrested by the Kempe Tai, jailed in Fort Santiago and badly beaten and starved. When I knew him, McCulloch-Dick was scabbed with sores, his flesh had shrunk on his bones, and his hands, feet and legs were bloated from beriberi. And yet, though he was past seventy, a life-lust seethed in the gnarled old Briton's veins. And the sparks that flew from the caves beneath his white, sprouting brows were touched off not so much by anger or irony as by a shrewd humor and tenacity. The Japanese had said that the old man was being left in the ward to die, but McCulloch-Dick would survive. "Ah, when you're as old as I," he was fond of saying, "then — you're too old to die."

Every day the men in the ward were on the lookout for me. "Is the boy coming today?" they would ask Father, hours before I arrived. For to these grizzled old men with their shabby pyjamas and sick-room odor, I was a youthful symbol of defiance.

2.

Toby, who was two years older than I, lived at the Ateneo with his mother. He was a clever, somewhat taciturn boy whose dialect was difficult for me to understand, and I felt a bit sorry for him, thinking he had a speech impediment. When he told me he was born in "Mrs. Sippi" I was astonished to discover that it was not a person but a place.

On the loggia that overlooked the Ateneo courtyard, six or seven women would gather round a battered rattan table, sitting in wicker chairs at tea time. They looked decidedly shabby-genteel compared with the empress of the tea table, a gigantic Negress named Mrs. Sanders who brewed her tea from ginger root, mint and old tea leaves. I have never seen a more majestic presence than Mrs. Sanders who, indeed, stood well over six feet tall. Her size absolutely amazed me, for I was still young enough to half believe in giants. Toby always had his eye on her.

Since Toby seemed considerably perplexed by Mrs. Sanders as we watched her pouring tea, I told him that she was "a lady of color," a dainty expression of my parents' which seems preposterous today. But Toby disagreed, shaking his head and drawling a reply: "Nah, she's a Nigrah — jez a giant niggah." At that age I knew neither the word "Negro" nor "nigger," but I loved learning new words. "She's jez a gee-i-ant niggah — a Nigroh," Toby carefully drawled, then dared me to go and ask her.

Despite Mrs. Sanders' overwhelming size, there was nothing forbidding about her. On the contrary, her manner was magnanimous and welcoming. And I, in any case, was not one to be shy with strangers.

So I ran up to the tea table where Mrs. Sanders presided, large and comfortable, a palm-leaf fan in her lap, as she was handing Father Hooley a cup of tea. When I popped my question at her, I had not got Toby's words quite straight and they came out garbled.

"Are you a giant Niggerno?"

Squeaks of consternation from the pallid ladies at tea.

"Such a rude brat!"

"Of all the nerve!"

Mrs. Sanders, on the other hand, burst into such a flood of laughter that she simply could not answer my question. Father Hooley blanched further and jumped up from his chair, knocking over his tea. He snatched hold of my wrist. Then his face went livid, except for his nose, which seemed to sharpen to a thin, pale point. The Irish priest pulled me off to a far corner of the courtyard saying that I ought to be sent forthwith back to the Children's Home where I would be disciplined and looked after.

Leaving me to cry and sulk in the corner, Father Hooley returned to his upset tea. As I glanced round for Toby, out of the tail of my eye I noticed that Mrs. Sanders had stood up to her huge height, had left her guests at tea and was advancing towards me in the full glare of the afternoon sun. When she loomed near, she drew out a handkerchief that she kept at her bosom and was soon offering it to me. She seemed so colossal in that harsh sunlight that I stood shrinking under her shadow, scarcely able to take in what she was saying. Mrs. Sanders bent over me, wiping my tears away with her handkerchief.

"Curiosity! That's all. You didn't mean any harm. No harm at all. Why, of all the ideas!"

Hesitantly, I gazed up at her massive face, up at her great sculptured bones, and straight into her eyes. Deep brown eyes they were, eyes that seemed to come from a long way back, from an old, old earth. She spoke all the while; she continued patiently talking to me as I looked up at the strays of her grey, crinkled hair that crept from beneath her red bandana; then I glanced down at the dark brown of her dress, which matched the warm darkness of her flesh. And I knew that there was no need to make explanations as she stood there, immense and serene, for she understood unspoken thoughts. Then, giving me her hand, she led me back to the loggia, saying, "From now on you call me Ma *Sawn-ders;* that's the way you say it. I'll fix things up for you. You wait and see."

At the tea table, a smile stretched liberally over Father Hooley's face, revealing a glint of Jesuitical teeth. Still with her hand holding mine, Mrs. Sanders seated herself in her tall, wickerwork chair and looked down at the priest.

"This boy is *not* going back to any Children's Home," she said firmly. Then she went on with a certain old nonchalant grandeur: "He's here so that he can creep through the hole in the fence and visit his folks. And *here* is where he's going to stay. And he *has* got somebody to look after him — because *I'm* going to do the looking after." Reaching for her palm-leaf fan, Mrs. Sanders drew the subject to a close, knowing that Father Hooley would not dare contradict her.

But Mrs. Sanders did not manage to do the looking after for long. Japanese orders came. In a few weeks' time I was sitting in a carromata on my way back to the Children's Home. The Imperial Army had requisitioned the Ateneo; I was the first to leave, and on the following day Mrs. Sanders and everyone else would be sent back to Santo Tomás.

"Don't you cry, baby mine," Mrs. Sanders had said, enfolding me in her enormous arms as she kissed the tears from my face. "Don't you cry. We're going to be together again, you'll see. Stop that crying, you hear? When this war is over, you're going to be the happiest boy in the world. And when you are, I want you to remember your old Ma Sanders."

With her kisses fresh upon my cheeks, I sat in the carriage, crushed between Father Hooley and a Japanese guard. We sat without saying a word as the horse clopped over the deserted streets towards the Pasig River. Ever since General Tojo's visit, a month earlier, the Japanese oppression weighed heavily over the land. Hunger was beginning to grow in Manila; people were stopped in the streets and searched; doors were broken down by rifle butts in the dead of night. Filipinos were arrested; Filipinos were shot. Often, in the mornings, the corpses of Japanese soldiers were found in the street, with knives in their backs.

3.

That evening at supper, back at the Children's Home, Sweeney hailed me and grinned. "Bastard's back," he announced for the benefit of the new Shanghai group at table. All through the meal he sat chuckling at his own jokes. "Wormy corny puddin' again." And the other boys tittered with that polite, uneasy laughter usually reserved for the jocularity of priests. But Sweeney was right. Food was scant now and bad. The boys had grown thinner, more restless and, as a result, much nastier.

Shortly after breakfast the next morning, Sister Sanctissima sailed into the dormitory to tell me, "Your yaya is here to see you." Terray! I scampered down the stairs with the mocking shrieks of the dormitory ringing in my ears. "Your yaya! Your yaya is here to see you!"

Terray brought notes from Father and Mother and another signed by all the men in the men's ward at Philippine General Hospital. She told me that Alfredo had returned to his home province of Illocos Norte — "to wait for when the Americans will come." So Alfredo had joined the guerrillas in the north!

"Is he with Looming, Terray?" But my question seemed to baffle her.

"Looming? No one can tell where is Looming. He run away when Japs come." Terray looked hastily at my feet. "See, bad boy, you never learn to tie shoes. Now you wear shoes no more."

Opening her straw handbag, Terray drew out a coconut-rice cake wrapped in banana leaf. "You eat this here," she said, pushing the cake into my mouth piece by piece. "See what I also bring? Music for happiness." When I saw what she had brought I nearly went sick, my mouth glutted with sweet coconut and rice. Terray pointed to my black portable gramophone, opened it and showed me a dozen of my favorite records. My eyes smarted; I began to choke. How could I explain that I didn't want them? How could I tell her to take them away?

Terray had turned her back to me. She fussed with her shawl, arranged the combs in her hair, then took up her market bag.

"You be good boy and do what teacher tells," she said, crossly.

I was nodding, mouth full and throat full. But it was Terray who began to cry.

"No more now. I go. Bye-bye." She gave me a desperate hug and fled out the door.

I never saw her again. When she went on her regular visit to my mother at the hospital, Terray was stopped by Japanese soldiers, taken to a guardhouse and questioned for twelve hours. To frighten her, they warned her that if she returned, they would take her baby away. From then on she smuggled food, money and clothing to Mother through one of the hospital orderlies.

Late in the dark, the voices of insomniac children kept each other company with the tales of the tortures at Fort Santiago. Sweeney would start the long night off with Fingernail Torture, telling us how information was extorted from a prisoner by pressing sharp, thin slivers of bamboo between the nail and the quick of the prisoner's fingers. Sweeney did not obtain his information direct from the source. He extracted torture stories with small gifts or the promise of friendship from some new boy, fresh with the latest tales from Santo Tomás. Occasionally, one of Sweeney's pets was pressed to tell a tale of torture himself.

"OK, let's hear about water torture from Homer Young. Tell it like ya told me, Homer."

A small voice would gulp and start.

"They get this guy, see? And they don't give him any water for three whole days. Then they make him stand up straight for six hours long, right on tiptoe. And all this time he's got to hold a great big bowl of nice cool water in his hands. If the guy gets dizzy — if the guy starts to faint or fall — up come the Japs with their bamboo sticks and go whack on his face, whack on his elbows, whack-whack on his knees."

"Tell 'em how they get the big bamboo stick jammed up the asshole."

If the lad fell asleep during his tale, Sweeney would crawl over to his bed and poke at him.

"C'mon now, Homer. Wake up! We wanna hear all about how they make 'em stand on red-hot coals and burn their feet."

And the drowsy kid would waken and try to finish the story, only to drop off again halfway through.

"No you *don't!*" Sweeney would warn. "I'm not gonna let you sleep till you tell about how they stomp on 'em with those great big hobnail boots."

We went to bed hungry every night, those whispering nights of rumors and torture stories. The early effects of malnutrition did not sap our strength so much as make us irritable and turn us into the victims of our fears. Only in the afternoons did these dark anxieties come rushing out into the open, to resolve themselves in children's games.

4·

War began at three o'clock. Directly Sister Holy Redeemer had dismissed us from class we scrambled downstairs and blustered rowdily into the yard. A shrill whistle from Sweeney. The scuffling stopped and everybody huddled anxiously round him while he divided us into sides. Sweeney called the rules of the game and the grubby flock of predatory boys awaited his commands. Then in his umpire voice Sweeney proclaimed whether it would be Americans against British, or Catholics against Protestants. The battle was sure to be in Sweeney's favor: Americans and Catholics formed the majority, and, unless outsmarted, his side always won.

War originated from our earlier games of Hide and Seek, which Sweeney had combined with Capture the Flag. Fear of the Japanese forbade the use of real flags, so a red polka-dot scarf made do for the Stars and Stripes and a banner cut from a blue plaid shirt stood for the Union Jack. White was the flag for truce or parley. There was no surrender.

First, a strategy caucus; then Sweeney sent both gangs off into hiding. At his Indian war whoop, scouts advanced and we were at war. The chief objective was to take as many captives as possible and drag them by the hair or by the ears to prison camp. Ordinarily, a squad of four tackled the first enemy soldier that appeared, twisted his arm behind his back and made him prisoner of war. But if you were alone, or your side was losing, you found a smaller fellow, threw dust in his eyes, stoned him till he cried and then took him captive. To catch a bigger boy, you hid up a tree and jumped behind him as he passed, gripping your arm tightly round his throat, driving your knee into the small of his back.

There was one queer turn to War: even if you captured the enemy flag, your side did not win. Flags, after all, could always be recaptured. It was a question of breaking morale. Not until every prisoner had succumbed to torture and joined the enemy ranks was the winning side declared.

No boy was exempt from War. Anyone who rebelled or evaded Sweeney's military conscription had the rabble on his back and soon learned what a real thrashing was. In War it was quite acceptable to be a bully or a cheat. Not so a coward. Cowards were cuffed, kicked down and stamped upon. I despised the game and several times disrupted it by frankly sitting in the centre of the yard, refusing to play.

"Get the Bastard! Beat him up!"

The pack would promptly be on top of me, making me grind my teeth on a mouthful of dirt.

"Do you give up, Bastard?"

As soon as I surrendered, they would let me go. But often, after I had caught my breath, I would recant. This drove the gang to such a pitch of fury that I would be made to surrender again. And though I had many sympathizers, not one dared defy Sweeney's henchmen. Instead, they coaxed and pleaded with me to play the game. Or at least pretend to. And in time I yielded.

When British Lions battled American Eagles, I fought alongside Derek and Chris Bure against the American birds of prey. Consequently my English accent became more pronounced in sheer defiance of Sweeney's Americanese. Since I was the only Catholic Briton, the brothers Bure were supposed to be my enemies when Sweeney switched to religious war — Capture the Cross. My friends were mostly Protestants, so I blithely turned traitor to Pope Sweeney.

On the other hand, whenever I battled for Britain in Capture the Flag, it galled me to kneel and kiss the ground before the feet of Sweeney's superpowered American legions. I refused to betray the British banner and was hauled off to prison camp where I had sticks prodded in my ears or armpits and frequently for good measure had my face ducked in a bucket of mud and worms.

For a while Capture the Flag assumed the cruder rudiments of fair play when Sweeney assigned a few Americans to fight for the Union Jack. These chaps were usually his pet peeves: snivellers, the cross-eyed, boys with buck teeth or boys who puked easily. Our most welcome recruits were lads who had incurred Sweeney's disfavor by using long words or interrupting him. Two were merely confusing cases: little Mees was sent to the British army because he was Dutch and Joel Stein because he was a Jew. Later, however, when Sweeney discovered that Christ too was a Jew, Joel became a Catholic in Capture the Cross.

With our troops enlarged, Britain won several battles. Sweeney was stung; he could not endure belonging to the losing side.

So the new crusades waged and raged for weeks until one day Hugh Carmichael set the Catholic across ablaze and carried the fiery emblem into the centre of the battlefield. Rocks hurled past, fairly grazing Sister Holy Redeemer as she bucked and sprinted over the battlefield trying to intervene. For penance we were banished from the garden and confined to the dormitory. Here we would remain until a games mistress could be sent from Santo Tomás.

5.

The Japanese authorities refused permission for me to visit my father in hospital, though I was allowed to see my mother twice. Neither of us knew in advance when these visits would take place. A Philippine Red Cross matron with an armband would suddenly come to fetch me in a carromata. There were Japanese sentry posts along the way and when we were halted, the matron handed them my pass.

On my second visit Mother had been removed to a narrow, darkened room with drawn blinds. When I entered the room she lay motionless and pale; her eyes were shut. I stepped forward silently, unable to believe what I saw: the hair had gone dull and was shredded with grey, the body had become wasted and the hands were stiffly folded over the sheet. SHE MUST BE DEAD. In hot and cold waves of terror, I drew closer to her, softly sounding the *M* in "Mother." She woke abruptly.

But panic became my master: for the first time I understood that my mother could die. Now it was no longer a neutral fact but something that I believed. I saw my mother stripped of her strength, emaciated and old. And I saw her terror too and, as it leapt out at me, it became our terror — hers and mine. It was the animal dread that lurks between each breath of our mortality. I could not brave it.

We talked together quietly, she in a faint, thin echo of her voice, with its familiar cadences, its music almost muffled. And I spoke weakly, frightened by her waxen face and by the shingles, those great blisters like grapes that covered her breast and throat. Mother went on murmuring while I sat in an iron chair, half-deaf, my knees gone soft, dread-possessed.

The Red Cross matron intruded; it was time for me to go. And my terror jumped frantically, turning me footloose, so that I went racing down endless hospital corridors — white, white ahead of me. I rushed headlong into whiteness, evading the hands of the nurses that stretched to catch me. Then, though I flung my flesh and bones against it, I was stopped by a hard, white wall. Behind me the nurses and orderlies were catching up; I was cornered. I would dissolve, but I could not. Instead I grew into a frightened, angry animal that was caught howling and shrieking, and fought to free itself from the starched white restraining figures.

Captured in this dragnet of hospital attendants, I was brought to the staff room and slapped by a nurse. A young Filipino doctor sent the nurse from the room. Then he sat on the table, a stethoscope round his neck.

"What do you want?" he asked.

A hoarse voice replied, "I want my mother."

More gently still, the doctor asked, "Why?"

"To care for me, so that I can care for her."

He continued speaking until I could stand up no longer and buckled to the floor, eyes so swollen with hot, silent tears that I was blind except to the light that shone red through my inflamed eyelids. Sounds of the door opening and closing as attendants came and went. I lay there until I grew calm beneath cold compresses, until the dread grew mute within me and reason mured up feeling. Then I rode dumbly back, oblivious of the Red Cross matron, of the streets, of Japanese sentries, and arrived once more at the Children's Home.

The Red Cross matron made certain that the details of my hospital visit reached everyone at the Home. Strangely, the other boys did not rag me. Even the nickname "Bastard" was suspended for a time. Sweeney was so quiet that the weary, sadistic crease at his mouth softened. His own mother was dead three years by then.

While reading of the battle between Wolf and Montcalm for Montreal, I came upon the quatrain from Gray's "Elegy Written in a Country Churchyard":

> The boast of heraldry, the pomp of pow'r
> And all the beauty, all that wealth e'er gave,
> Awaits alike th' inevitable hour:
> The paths of glory lead but to the grave.

These words awakened the tragic sense in me, a sense nurtured by my mother, which had slept in the deep underconscious. The tragic sense is a stronger, sterner master than dread. It may be understood but it cannot be explained. I memorized the entire "Elegy."

6.

We were growing restless and morose up in the dormitory. Five days of banishment seemed long enough. Our bones stiffened with boredom; eventually everyone began to droop, to yawn and drowse through the humid day.

Then the sun disappeared. A foreboding twilight had been

gathering through the morning and by noon the darkness settled; the air was close and damp. We looked out into the gloomy garden and saw that the leaves on the trees were folded over. The wind sprang up and the trees began to flutter and sway. From far away we heard a heavy rumbling. Not bombs or cannon but thunder. Overhead the black sky went churning, opened suddenly to reveal infinities of angry platinum, then blacked out again. Through the lightning flashes we watched the wind wrestling with trees; it bent them to right angles and stripped them of their leaves. Silence. Big spots of rain and the rising odor of wetted earth. And the spates came sheeting down like Niagara, gorging waterspouts, conduits, sewers, relentlessly thrashing the lanes of the Holy Ghost, gushing away plants, flailing the trees under the compulsion of the wind.

At midnight boys woke, wet and shouting; the typhoon raged at the windows and water flushed through the sills.

"Close the windows!" But the windows were shut.

"Switch on the lights!" But the electric current had failed. Then the latch on a window gave way and the storm swung in.

"Tear a sheet — tie it down!"

The boys battled to hold the storm back, fastened the window, pushed beds towards the central passageway until the room grew into a dim white forest of mosquito nets. By morning the torrents had turned the garden to mud and ooze. Manila was in the typhoon's centre. The sea level rose, and nearby, the Pasig River (hidden from our view by Malacañang Palace) was in high water.

Nuns in their black habits moved among us, confident that God would keep His promise to Noah and the world would never again be destroyed by the waters of a flood. Sister Holy Redeemer spoke of a dove bearing a branch from an olive tree.

The Pasig River overflowed its banks. And the flood tide came rushing towards us, filling the streets of Manila. The garden, once our battlefield, became a lake that grew and inundated the kitchen of the Children's Home. Outside, the streets were rapidly flowing canals. Houses floated away. People were drowned.

"God is punishing the Japanese," said Sister Sanctissima.

By the third day, the worst of the storm passed over. Through parting clouds, the sun briefly appeared and glowered at the water, which had risen to a depth of five feet and more. From the infirmary window we looked down to the street at destitute Filipino families punting along Calle Mendiola on makeshift bamboo rafts. Steps drifted by and the bloated body of a horse. Boards, furniture and rubbish were caught in eddies of the brown, filthy water reeking of tropic rot. In our building, centipedes and scorpions came out from their secret places, and great ravenous rats as well.

Sweeney organized vigilantes to go sneaking down the corridors and beat the rats dead with a broom. We formed squadrons to bail out water and keep mopping up. When little Mees discovered a scorpion in his suitcase, I fetched the prayerbook from the sister's desk and crushed the venomous brute.

The flood became an emergency more immediate, more specific than the world at war. Rain seeped through sills and walls; dampness lingered in the atmosphere — our beds were damp, our clothes and even the pages of our books. In the beginning we had greeted the flood as an adventure, but now that the typhoon had passed over, our fears struggled to unleash themselves — for the waters still were rising. And yet the flood had also worked a change in the boys at the Children's Home. The fights and the bullying, the rivalries and jealousies had vanished. We began to get on with one another. Lads who had once gone for each other's throats found themselves side by side fighting the flood instead. For two years Sweeney had used his powers to turn a roomful of boys against each other, watching them vie for his favors. Quite suddenly his motives altered course. Sweeney no longer seemed so eager to remain absolute dictator. Perhaps he felt trapped in the game he had instigated but was not quite able to win. In any case, when the flood gave him opportunity to save face, he made good use of it.

7.

Shortly after the flood, we had learned that a Miss Bullpin was being sent from Santo Tomás to be our games mistress. She came of a family of acrobats, we were told, which had been billed as a circus act called "The Twirling Bulls." Although the name of her act sent us into a riot of smutty puns, we were immediately disposed in her favor. A real circus acrobat! We expected the extraordinary and our suspense mounted till the day she arrived.

Sister Sanctissima released us from our lessons that afternoon, announcing that Miss Bullpin awaited us in the yard. We clattered downstairs in a rush, though the gang slackened pace at the sight of her.

Muscular and tall, Miss Bullpin stood in the middle of the yard, her rather dirty man's shirt rolled up at the sleeves. Unkempt sorrel hair straggled to her shoulders like skeins of tangled wool. The circus lady wore khaki trousers and some sort of cowboy boots. Her eyes were as keenly taunting as her manner was rough and ready. Miss Bullpin swaggered towards us bouncing a soccer ball.

"Okey-dokey, boys," she said, dispensing with introductions, "we're gonna play soccer."

Before anyone had time to think, the lads found themselves caught in the thick of a swift game of soccer. I was the only one to mutiny.

"Sorry, I don't play games."

"Shut up, smarty-pants!" she squawked in a voice suggesting Texarkana.

"Mind your manners and your tone of voice," I ordered.

Miss Bullpin took me by the ear and twisted it sharply. Without a second's hesitation I turned round and fetched her a ringing smack in the face. She sent me flying into the game with her terrific, well-aimed kick.

It was soccer for me that day.

The other lads had mixed feelings about the lady acrobat. In the course of the game several others had been tweaked, knocked about and hurtled into position. But young boys often have an odd respect for rough treatment, and then too Miss Bullpin had organized a smashing game of soccer. For my own part, she seemed blood-brother to the Japanese officer who had clouted my mother when we arrived at Santo Tomás. The rest of the lads eyed me with grave misgivings: one did not strike an adult.

Soccer and the circus lady ruled the afternoons for several days. But before long, undernourishment and restless sleep had sapped our energies and any respect for our hardy Miss Bullpin gave way to unanimous dislike. She made a habit of tripping lads whom she found sluggish or reluctant, then chuckling with self-satisfaction as she watched them sprawl. She had not, however, reckoned on Sweeney.

Alas for the circus lady, Sweeney felt sullen one sultry afternoon: he was in no mood for rapid soccer. She put out her foot to trip him, but this time did not laugh. Maintaining his balance and altar-boy poise, Sweeney gave her a long, incredulous look. He spoke very quietly, though he spoke between his teeth.

"Nobody ever does that to me."

Hastily, the boys rallied round him in alarm.

"Did she try and trip *you*, Sweeney?"

Meantime, Miss Bullpin was chasing Hugh Carmichael, and we heard the dangerous Scotch lad roar, "Keep away from me, ye dairty bitch!"

Miss Bullpin was no match for Hughie if she got his anger roused. I called out from a safish distance, "Best mind your manners, Bullpin. I shan't warn you again."

"Where's the snot that piped up?"

Arms akimbo, the acrobat hiked towards me. Joel Stein blocked her way. Taking him by the hair, she said in her best wise-guy manner, terse as Mae West and tougher than Cagney, "Better start playin' ball, boy."

She pushed him and he fell.

"Awright, fellas, nobody play. Hear me? She isn't gonna push Joel around."

Sweeney had called the strike. And the whole gang was chanting:

> Go away! Go away!
> Bullpin, go away.
> We won't play
> With you today.

"Where's the ringleader — ? Lemme get my hands on him!"

Sweeney was too swift. He darted out of her reach, crying, "Quick fellas. Up to the dorm!" And the pack followed fast at his heels.

We bolted up the stairs at the pitch of excitement. War had never been so good as this. As soon as we were in the dormitory, we barricaded the door with our beds and luggage. Sweeney was leaning out of the window shouting down to Dame Bull, as he called her:

"Keep outa the boys' dorm. Or we'll beat the pants off you!"

We massed at the windows, vociferously warning her to keep away from our dorm. She stood square in the sunlight, her sleeves rolled up for the fray, brandishing her fist. And then to our bewilderment she turned and went tramping off in the opposite direction. We waited. No sign of her. So we stationed little Mees at the window to keep watch while we settled down to a game of marbles on the floor. Quite a long time passed before the Dutch voice of Mees called us from our game.

"She comes — with a tree!"

As we boys jumped up to man our towering barricade, Sweeney's whistle put a stop to any noise. We held our breath and listened. We heard the stump of her cowboy boots on the stair; each stump was followed by a thud. Stump, thud, stump, thud — she was up to the stairs by now and coming down the corridor. Stump, thud, stump. We stood at attention. Then the thud began to butt at our door. Some luggage from the top of the barricade fell to the floor. There was the rattle of the doorknob turning, and as the door came open a crack, several beds and desks gave way.

Miss Bullpin screeched through the crack at the door:

"Get ready! I wanna see you squirts fight. Yeah! I wanna fight, see? I'm gonna fight the bunch of you. Wanna fight you — one by one!"

"Keep out, Dame Bull!"

"Say that agin, Bull-bitch. I dinna hear ye clear!"

All through the caterwaul, Miss Bullpin kept thudding at the door. Suddenly the pile of beds, mattresses and desks came toppling and clattering down. A round of boyish laughter: we had seen her battering ram — the roots of a tree.

In she came, her hair woolly and wild, her face flushed with bravado, as she wielded an eight-foot papaya tree — leaves, roots and all. Athletically, Miss Bullpin romped over the beds, desks, mattresses and luggage from our toppled barricade; then using the tree as a pole, she vaulted to the top of the sister's table.

"Okey-dokey, who's the punk that said he's gonna beat me up?"

She capered about on the table, holding the papaya tree upright so that it resembled an oversized umbrella.

"Aw c'mon — I wanna fight. Gonna take you on — one by one."

Hughie was closest to her. She diddled the tree at him; she called him a coward and guffawed. Reddened with wrath, Hughie crouched low and sprang at her. Standing on the top of the table, Miss Bullpin plunged the roots of the tree full in his groin. Hughie groaned; he retreated doubled over. I rushed at the tree sideways and grappled with it.

"OK, you guys, back the Bastard up!" came the Sweeney voice.

The boys charged at the tree and we had Tug-o'-War. It was yo-ho-heave-ho. Try again. Yo-ho-heave-ho! Almost got it. YO-HO — HEAVE — HEAVE —— HO! And we wrenched it from her.

She stood on the table, stunned. She was stripped of her weapon.

"Out of this room at once!" I called.

The lady acrobat bounded from the table; her hands were outstretched. Hunched like an enraged gorilla, she swung towards me and got me by the throat. Then Hughie swept to his revenge. He jumped to the table and took her from behind — just as we had done in War. Driving his knee into the acrobat's back and throttling her with his arm, the strapping Highlander mastered her. She let go my throat.

With Hughie clamped to her back, she sprang to her feet and heaved luggage this way and that. The room turned from uproar to riot. Every boy in the dormitory was tackling her. She was down on the floor; she wrestled herself free; she slugged. Sweeney tripped her and she sprawled. Again the gang was on top of her; soon she was being dragged, struggling, towards the door.

A piercing squeal from little Mees. Blood! Miss Bullpin had bitten his arm.

Every man Jack of us was lashed to a fury. The circus lady was being carried to the window like a struggling fly by a troop of angry red ants. At the windowsill, the Bure brothers and I intervened. We insisted that she be given her last chance: would she give over and leave our room?

"Ain't one of you geek-freaks is ever gonna make me give up!" And she kicked and she spat and she scratched herself free. "Lemme take you on — one by one!"

The scrimmage started up again; she was being forced head-first out of the window. Through the brabble of boys and Bull-pin's yelps came Sweeney's hard and husky soprano: "One . . . two . . . three!"

In a trice Miss Bullpin was over the windowsill and chucked out of the room. Smash! A dead pause. A nervous flutter among us as we jostled each other, craning our necks, each anxious to have a look. Had we hurt her?

"Why you Goddamn pansy-assed, shit-in-the-pants, prick-piss-ing patsys . . ." came the voice of Miss Bullpin.

She had landed on the tarpaper kitchen roof, almost a dozen feet below, smack on her bum.

Thanks to the bite on little Mee's arm, the affair ended quite simply. Miss Bullpin would be returned to Santo Tomás.

On the day of her departure we were admonished by the nuns to apologize. We felt, however, that an apology was due to us instead. So we made our protest by sweetly shaking her hand and piping in choir-boy voices:

"I'm sorry, Miss Bull."

"Bullpin," Sister Sanctissima corrected, primly.

8.

Along with the flood, this bizarre incident pulled us closer to-gether. Two years of Sweeney's dictatorship and War in the afternoon gave way to a new era. My own part as the first to rebel against soccer and the acrobat had won me an honorary membership in this new regime of comradeship. Up until now I had made the impression of a little Lord Fauntleroy and a recalcitrant snob. My haughty airs had won out. My refusal to yield to authority — whether Sweeney, the mob or Miss Bullpin — had gained acceptance for me on my own individual and eccentric terms. And we had all learned to make allowance for each other's differences of taste, nationality and background.

But this Utopia was doomed before it could be tested by time. By early December a large number of war prisoners was transferred from Santo Tomás to the Los Baños Camp, far south of Manila. Soon it was Christmas week and while we sang "The hopes and fears of all the years," the earliest, uncertain rumors came that the Children's Home would be shut down.

On New Year's Eve, after lights-out at eight o'clock, we sat up in our beds singing "Daddy Let Me Stay Up Late" as we waited for midnight and 1944. There was a lull in our singing. Then from far away we heard another song and the distant voices of men. We thought that the singing came from Santo Tomás, about a mile away. The faint voices mounted in the melancholy night until we recognized "Where the nightingales are singing and a white moon beams." At midnight, at the year's turning, the remote voices started the next stanza, and this time, fervent and slow, we joined in their singing until the night swelled with our song:

> There's a long, long night of waiting
> Until my dreams all come true,
> Till the day when I'll be going down
> That long, long trail with you . . .

Our voices faltered; no one knew the rest of the words, and while a few of us hummed the tune, others dropped asleep or lay there quivering with hopes and fears, trying to imagine our rescue, which must surely come in this New Year. Presently only Sweeney and I were awake.

"Hey, Bastard, you still there?"

"Yes, Sweeney, what is it?"

"You know, I jus' figured somethin' out. When your mother's

dead, she's dead forever. And there's nobody who's ever gonna take her place."

"Well, we're probably getting too old for mothers anyway. Don't you think so, Sweeney?"

"Yeah . . . Do you feel older'n ten years old too?"

"Ages older. Fifteen, at least."

"An' I figured out somethin' else too. This is gonna be the last war in the world. Y'know why? Because when we win, there won't be any country left for us to fight." And as we continued talking, we both felt so sorry for each other, so sorry for ourselves and so brave. Neither of us knew how lucky we were, even then.

Late on a Sunday afternoon, just as we were coming from Benediction service in the chapel, I was told that someone had come to see me. I do not remember my visitor's name. He was a young Filipino in his mid-thirties. He had heard that the Children's Home would close within the week.

"Your papa and mama will stay in the hospital. So when you are in Santo Tomás, you will be all alone."

I thought that he might be a friend of my father's from the Jockey Club.

"No, I have never met your papa. But I have seen him many times when he was judge on the grandstand at San Lazaro," he replied. Then he gave a short laugh. "Always I lost money in the races."

The stranger's tone changed; he was in a hurry and had several errands before curfew and nightfall. Quickly he drew a small, flat parcel from his coat. It was wrapped in brown paper and tied with string.

"You take this and open it later. In Santo Tomás you will have need of it."

My Filipino friend had gone. I remained in the convent reception room, unwrapping the parcel. Money! Mickey Mouse money in every conceivable kind of note. Two hundred pesos!

I'd never seen so much money before. I wrapped it up carefully, slipped it inside my shirt, then, when I was back in the dormitory, hid it in my suitcase.

On Thursday, February tenth, we climbed up into a Japanese Army van and were off to Santo Tomás. As we plunged ahead in the warm, rough wind, skies were fair and my spirits soaring. I looked forward to adventure, to being alone in the camp and without adult supervision. The rest of the boys were glad to be going back to their families in camp. I glanced over at Sweeney who would soon be with his father and elder sister. His jade-green eyes were pert; five brown freckles stippled the snub of his nose. And he sang:

> There'll always be an England,
> There'll always be a France,
> There'll always be a big, big hole
> In Hitler's underpants.

The Scots lads broke in lustily:

> There'll always be an England
> So long as Scotland stands!

We bumped towards Santo Tomás, then stopped outside the Main Gate. We could not see inside. The gate, as well as the wrought-iron bars around the camp, were covered with matting of split bamboo so that the prisoners were screened from view. Japanese soldiers swung the gate open, shouting orders to the truck drivers. The boys sniggered when one of the soldiers opened his fly and pissed. Our van pulled in past the Main Gate and halted before a small shed. As we clambered down from the back of the truck, the soldier buttoned up his trousers and paddled off to another guard. They slammed the gate shut behind us.

At the Inspection Shed, a cheery soldier with a shaven head fancied my little black gramophone. I made no protest lest he discover my money, which was stitched to the seat of my shorts. Nor did he find my camera, which I had wrapped in clothing and hidden in two pieces in my suitcase. I kept the camera throughout the war. It was my secret, my childish act of defiance as a prisoner of war.

III

Back to Santo Tomás

The Kindness of Mr. Ohashi

1.

NIGHT IN THE GYMNASIUM was a din of incessant snores, coughs, groans, the throttled cries of nightmares and the sound of a low voice moaning. I dreamed that I was in a Pullman berth high in the Canadian Rockies: the train gathers speed in the night, its whistle echoing in the valleys and tunnels below. I woke up and scratched the mosquito bite on the back of my neck. The moon at the windows was casting bars of shadows over the Gymnasium; somewhere close by, a rat rummaged in an old man's luggage. I drowsed back to sleep for a moment, then drifted awake again. Too-hoot! Hoo-oot! I had been wakened by the whistling sleeper in the bed beside me.

The Gym, the largest dormitory in Santo Tomás, resembled an emergency hospital hastily thrown together in the midst of a typhoid epidemic. About three hundred men slept here, huddled together with only an arm's length between.

The men in the Gym were aged fifty or over, and, in fact, the male population of Santo Tomás consisted mostly of older men and young boys, the greater number of able-bodied men having been sent to Los Baños. The stench in the cavernous Gym was heavy and sickly sweet — I gagged when I first was ushered here. Even when I was out of the building the odor still clung to my body.

John Roy Shaw, an old friend of my father's, also lived in the

Gymnasium; he was now in his seventies. Before the war
Uncle John had been an enormous man who had wined and
dined on only the best for over forty years. Prison camp had
made him barely recognizable: flesh hung in folds on men
who had once been fat and Uncle John looked like a burst
paper bag. I had taken a special liking to him, for I remembered
hearing my mother say he despised children. Since I refused to
consider myself a child, we got on famously. I used to fetch
drinking water for him and loved to listen to him talk. Uncle
John Shaw had a large pocket watch of engraved gold that no
longer kept the time, though its bell could strike if it were set.
As he talked he would take out the watch, shake it absent-
mindedly and set the alarm. His conversation was of ocean
liners, of grand hotels, especially of banquets and their bills of
fare. He was also extremely precise about dates:

"In Paris, during the summer of 1909, we dined at Foyot's
on *canard à l'orange*. Some will tell you that it is a heavy meal
for mid-July — I disagree. It was the very finest duck I'd had.
However, when we stopped at Raffles Hotel in January of 1924,
I found their duck with mango superior. Mind you, of late
years, I hear that the art of cuisine in Singapore is not what it
has been . . ."

The entire camp had bedbugs — even Uncle John — and many
of us had lice. In the daytime we were fretted by flies, plagues
of flies hissing and bustling about, hungrily trying to alight on
an eye or a nose to find a morsel to feed on.

No one could escape from the LOUDSPEAKER. It reached the
farthest corners of the camp and governed our action through
the day. At sunrise it would burst out as the needle struck
the groove of a worn recording, often of a trio of girls crooning "Good Morning," which played so loudly that the words
were indistinct. Then, like the staccato rasps of Hitler played
backwards, came the Nipponese blasting orders to their sentries. An American voice followed, a radio voice washed in

soapsuds, bubbling with folksy familiarity as it gave us our orders for the day. At ten- or twenty-minute intervals the LOUDSPEAKER would switch suddenly on, ordering someone to report to the commandant's office, repeating the order, giving instructions to labor squads, repeating the instructions, paging doctors and telling mothers to fetch their children from begging the Japanese soldiers for food.

Other boys had parents to curb their truant tendencies but I, although expected to attend school in the mornings, more often wandered the camp. Just behind the Main Building stood the camp kitchen. In one of the two open sheds were rough-hewn wooden benches and tables at which the women on kitchen detail sat picking insects and stones out of rice, chopping up greens and paring camotes (yams which had once been eaten only by the mountain tribes in hunger months). They also cleaned fish. The fish were finger-sized. They had been dynamited in schools and the dead-stinkers and poisonous fish had to be carefully removed from the more edible ones.

As I strolled past the women's work shed on a sultry mid-afternoon, a deep contralto called out after me, "Why, honey child! Baby! Yes, baby — I mean YOU! Come on over here. I've been looking for you."

And there she was, in an old rayon dress that had once been navy-blue but was now bleached to a weirdly mottled purple by time and the tropic sun. Old Ma Sanders! Gigantic, she came over to me and engulfed me with those great, sagging arms. Then the floodgates burst and my whole body shook with gasping sobs. And Ma Sanders held me closer to her warm, wasting flesh, rocking me to and fro, asking no questions as she repeated over and over those words of comfort, those foolish reassurances that make the heart grow strong and glad.

So I sobbed and sobbed as I had not done in many months, not since I had visited my mother in hospital and thought she was dead. I was no longer a grown-up but instead a lonely boy sobbing out the six months of suppressed tears. And when the storm was almost over, my eyes met hers — they were dark and glowing in her old, big-boned face, as wise as the earth. For Ma Sanders *was* old, three score years and ten, she said. Seventy years of hope and sorrow shone openly in that face. Again I dissolved, but this time into such a salty bathos that the hiccups came. Old Ma began shaking with laughter while I hiccuped and laughed too until, cured even of hiccups, I laughed and she laughed, quite as long and loudly as I had cried.

Presently Ma Sanders set me to work peeling camotes. "You come here every day and work right here with me," she said. "Watch that camote, baby. Don't you peel it too thin — we're going to *eat* those leftovers!" We were allowed to keep some of the peelings, Ma explained, and the rest would be sold to the scavenger line to provide funds for the camp needy. Ma Sanders and I always made big peelings so that we could shave away the skins and cook the slivers — we had to pare off the skins for fear of dysentery.

"Sugar baby!" Old Ma called me when she discovered that I had paid a camp racketeer fifty pesos for two cups of brown sugar. "Well, you aren't going to do that again, honey child. From now on I'm going to do all your buying for you. No racketeer ever put anything over on me — I know how to bargain."

Old Ma Sanders and I took our meals together every day. We filtered peanut oil from the grinder when we made peanut butter for the scavenger line, and we used the oil to fry our peelings in. Then she bought us extra rice that she roasted on her Filipino clay-pot stove, which she stoked with dry twigs and thrifty bits of charcoal. Our parings rounded out the skimpy rations we received three times a day. Most prisoners in Santo Tomás had, by this time, lost at least thirty pounds in weight.

At our work one day, Ma kept glancing at me, knitting her brows and saying "Ah-hum" to herself. Then leaning over, she took a good look at my head and announced, "Honey, you've got lice!" Bidding me wait for her, she went off to her room and returned with a little flask of kerosene.

"Follow me." She beckoned with the air of a prophetess. "We're going to the laundry troughs out back of the Annex."

When we got there, she sat me up on a box, muttering, "Nits, lice," while she soaked my shaggy brown hair with the kerosene.

"Smells like a paraffin lamp," I complained.

"That's right, same thing," murmured Ma, absorbed in her task. "And you can't get it for money in this camp. Only for love."

The fluid seared at my scalp.

"Let me know if it burns; when it starts to burn it's got to be all washed out."

For days afterwards my head was on fire.

Save for a wide stretch of acacia trees before the Main Building and the Gate, the camp grounds had sprouted with vegetable gardens and patches, every other bit of space being occupied by clusters of shabby huts, known as Shanty-town. Between the far edges of Shanty-town and the matting-covered railing that enclosed the camp was a Japanese guard with a tic, who called everyone "Joe." One day he winked me over to him.

"You buy pork-chicken from me, Joe? I bring him to you."

My two hundred pesos were nearly spent, and since Ma did my bargaining for me, I decided to ask her advice. So I told the guard that I would come back in the afternoon.

Prisoners, of course, were strictly forbidden to traffic with guards. Old Ma Sanders frowned deeply when I told her about the offer. "Sounds pretty dangerous to me," she mused. Then she brightened quickly. "But it *would* mean something more to eat."

I did not wish Ma to deal with the guard. Children had never been punished by the Japanese, and since my parents were not in camp, they could not be reprimanded. It would be safer for me to try my luck alone.

"All right, if you want to. But don't you buy any pork. It

takes too long to cook and could make you sick — trichinosis. Try and get a chicken — but don't you pay more than fifteen pesos, and that's all. Start bargaining at ten."

Later in the day I went back to my guard.

"You, Joe, you want him pork-chicken?"

"I want chicken. How much?"

The Japanese guard held up both hands, twice. Twenty pesos. I held my hands signalling ten.

"No good, Joe. Chicken not cheap. Ten-ty."

"I don't have twenty pesos — fifteen."

The guard's face gave a tic. "No good, Joe. You buy ten-ty."

I decided to give in. "Yes. Twenty pesos."

"Pay money now, Joe. Tomorrow bring chicken."

"I pay money when you bring chicken."

"No good, Joe. No chicken."

"Very good. Here — twenty pesos."

"Damn fool," Ma Sanders called me. "You're never going to see that chicken."

Next day I went back to the Japanese guard.

"Too bad, Joe. No chicken. Tomorrow."

On the morrow I was told, "Go way, Joe. No chicken today."

The third day, my hopes undaunted, I returned to my guard again and still there was no chicken in sight. He, however, was all tic and smiles.

"Hello, Joe. I got him chicken."

Going over to a thicket, he brought out one live chicken from a wire cage, handling it by its feet. Having never held a chicken before I very nearly strangled it when the hen tried to peck at me. Grasping it grimly by the neck, I hastened off to the laundry troughs where Ma awaited me.

Upon seeing the scrubby creature, old Ma put her hands to her hips and burst out laughing. "Land's sakes, that sure is a pretty slim bird!" she said. "Come on, baby, I can't kill a chicken and neither can you. So we're going to find Mr. Connor who keeps an axe."

Off we went into the muddy depths of Shanty-town where Mr. Connor had built himself a hut of old boards, bamboo and nipa thatching. He proudly produced the contraband axe which he kept hidden under the shack. The execution, however, Ma Sanders absolutely refused to let me witness, although I had seen Alfredo behead a chicken and once, in fascinated terror, watched a headless hen trot round in circles till it fell. "Heavenly days! You aren't going to see anything like that with me, I do declare," Ma exclaimed with a fastidious shudder. "Besides, I hate the sight of blood and the sound of the poor thing cackling, so you'd better keep me company."

Later, Ma Sanders plucked the hen while I ground kernels of Indian corn to dredge the chicken in. Then we fried it in our pilfered peanut oil.

"Mighty tough bird for twenty pesos," proclaimed old Ma Sanders as we munched at its bones.

2.

Life was much harder now. Until 1944 Santo Tomás was under the administration of Japanese civilians. By this time the Imperial Army had taken absolute control of the camp. Pedlars were no longer allowed within our gates. Filipinos were prohibited from aiding us in any way. Although food could still be bought in the Manila markets, we in Santo Tomás were forbidden to buy it. Even the rich, unless they had hoarded tinned food, were feeling the pains of hunger. When Swiss, Swedish and other businessmen of the neutral community offered to donate funds to stave off slow starvation in our prison camp, the Imperial Japanese Army bluntly refused.

"I've seen a lots of hard times in my life," Ma Sanders would say, shaking her head, "and I tell you that I can see we're moving into the *hard*, hard times."

There was no sign of an American landing. Surely we had been forgotten: What did four thousand civilians in Santo

Tomás matter among the millions who were homeless, wounded, starving and slaughtered in the vaster prison of the world at war?

The afternoon was humid and close without a whisper of wind. No fish to clean; no camotes to peel. I sat glumly while Ma Saunders fanned me with the tatters of her palm-leaf fan. She looked at me, concerned. "What's the matter with you today? You're not talking. Must be something really wrong with you if *you're* not talking."

I twisted and hedged; I didn't feel like talking — besides, what was there to talk about? Ma went on studying my face; then she stretched out her hand and felt my forehead.

"I knew it. You have fever."

This I found ridiculous and fussy. "I don't have a fever. Just a sore throat."

Old Ma Sanders had pulled herself up and was standing over me like a pyramid. "Honey child, I know a fever. I know a fever when I see it and when I feel it."

"Go to hell!" I shouted at her, jumping up on the bench. "Who do you think you are — my mother?"

She seemed to pay no attention to this outbrust; she simply sat down again and, with that imperial nonchalance of the hand, she picked up her fan. When at length she spoke, her tone was casual.

"If you say you're not sick, you ought to know. But it sure does look to me like you have fever. Now if I were you — and maybe not feeling so good — I'd go over to the Isolation Hospital and have them take a look at you. There's lots of measles, lots of whooping cough and lots of chicken pox going around. You ever had them?"

My throat was awfully raw now; it seemed as though Ma had made it worse by mentioning it. I came down from the bench saying that perhaps I should go and lie down for a bit. As soon as I stepped out of the shade of the kitchen shed, the glare struck hard on my eyes. I felt cold and faint and was breaking into a sweat. The day was dead-white; the air refused to stir.

Suddenly the LOUDSPEAKER shouted over the camp: "Attention, please. The list for the Los Baños transfer is now complete. The day and time of departure will be included in a later announcement." The LOUDSPEAKER repeated itself.

Ma Sanders sat there in the shade; she had kept watching me all the while, still holding her tattered fan. As I hesitated and began to turn back towards her, she appeared to be so far away. Time seemed to have slackened as I made my way through the vast space of hostile light and back into the shade of the kitchen shed. The words stuck in my throat, but I admitted, "Yes, Ma — I really do feel ill."

We went off, hand in hand, behind the central kitchen and towards the Isolation Hospital. My head ached in the blinding sun; only her voice broke the hot stillness. "I can't go in there with you," Ma was saying. "Anyway, you're always telling me that you're grown-up, so I guess you'll be able to go in by yourself."

Old Ma Sanders looked miserably tired as she put her great, worn hand on my brow and wiped the sweat away. We had stopped at the hospital door and stood still. After a second's silence the weariness dropped from her face like a mask. She had raised that patient, massive face; she was gazing from the past, beyond the present and future, into the heart of a mythical kingdom. And her gaze defied boundaries, even our prison camp. She had always understood my boyish, willful independence, and she knew that some part of us could never be jailed, would never be explained; she knew that the human urge for freedom leaps and laughs at walls and cannot be confined by prison or reason. She was part of the motherly earth and understood the hard facts of the earth, its mysteries, for they lived within her — birth and death, the spring and the fall of things, happiness and sorrow: those eternal vanishings.

3.

Memory blurs as I move out of the blistering sun and enter
the shadows of hospital . . . Doctors come and go, figures seen
through the mist of my mosquito net. I can hear the words
"diphtheria," "slide," "smear" and then the fever submerges
me, sucking my memory with it . . . Military nurses from Bataan, women built like soldiers, clad in khaki shirts and trousers.
The night lamp thrusts their shapes over the ceiling above me
— I cannot distinguish the passing days from the nights that follow them. A nurse is standing before me, erect as an adjutant
with a message: "Some nigger lady came to tell you goodbye.
Says she's being transferred. She's going to the other camp —
Los Baños."

Weeks have faded into the grey zone of this twilight. A doctor says that I am getting better. Daylight is stealing through
the slats in the bamboo blinds; I begin to walk about, to go to
the lavatory. And I can hear the LOUDSPEAKER echoing through
the camp.

But I have taken ill again. Fever and the desire to sleep and
sleep. The hulking forms of soldier-nurses pass back and forth.
"Now you got measles, boy."

From sleep to waking: shadows move on the ceiling, the
nurses in khaki uniforms are shifting to and fro outside my
mosquito net. My rash looks lavender in the dusky light. When
I get out of bed the room begins to turn, faster, faster; the urinal
is in my hand and the floor melts under me . . .

Rain on the roof. Sweats. Chills. And coughing. My coughs
resound like fits of jeering laughter in this sunless place . . .
I shall shut my eyes tight until I can see stars and I shall pray.
Perhaps if I pray long enough, hard enough, the coughing will
stop. No. It starts up again and again. "Guess wut? Buddy's
got whooping cough. Yeah."

Pain knifes my chest. Violent chills. Mad dreams. And then I float out into the sea of forgotten time. . . . They have taken my temperature; I waken as they pull the greased thermometer out of my rectum. Soaked. The bedclothes are soaked in sweat . . . I can scarcely lift my hand . . . "He's OK, Doc. The kid's pulled through."

Hate. Hate them. They don't even know my name: Kid, Boy, Buddy. I am in . . . Isolation . . . Hospital. Ma Sanders has gone. I am alone in Santo Tomás. War prisoner. Mother and Father must be dead: both have deliberately died and left me. Not their real child, anyway. Adopted bastard brat.

I have spat the food all over the sheets; my face is ringing from the slap of that big military nurse. Now they force-feed me with a spoon. Choke, swallow . . . and then soundly sleep.

Golden as candlelight — Wake up to my name — Robin. Awake to a vision: bright, golden, curly hair. She calls me by name — Robin. She is dressed in white and holds half a glass of milk out to me. Her black eyes are fire-bright; the corners of her lips are sweetly curling into a little smile. She is very petite and speaks in a Russian accent.

"Please drink? Milk is so precious. It must not be wasted."

"Let me alone. I want to die."

She sits at my bedside, her curly hair all golden in the lamp-light.

"You want to die? Oh yes, naturally, yes." Her voice is soft and low, a yearning Russian voice. "For why should we live in this world? How coarse it is! How brutal!" She wrinkles her nose. "Life is cruel; death is kind." And her pretty mouth makes a pout. "Still, if you are going to die, how sinful to let you die alone! Let me sit here and hold your hand until you die."

Her tiny hand takes mine. And the overtones of her melancholy voice are chiding, faintly mocking as she exclaims, "*Ach! Bozhe moy!* How much you have suffered. Three dreadful diseases of childhood. And did you have pneumonia, after? *Gospodi!* I think nobody — nobody else has ever known such misfortune!" Tears fill her eyes; she averts her face. "And only eleven years old? A tragedy!"

"Who — are you?" I ask, drowsy but verging on giggles.

"Lilia Yelena. I come here to volunteer. My son has a funny nickname — we call him 'Cowbell.' "

"What time is it, Lilia?"

"Past midnight . . ."

I woke in the morning and drank the slightly soured milk.

4.

Two stretcher bearers arrived at the Isolation Hospital and carried me off, past the bathhouses behind the Education Building, beyond the edges of Shanty-town and into the Santa Catalina Hospital, which adjoined the camp grounds. This was the main hospital, equipped during the more lenient first year of the Japanese occupation. A far cry from the Isolation Hospital, Santa Catalina was not a place where I was cut off from life and death. And there were no soldier-nurses to call me Kid, or Buddy or Boy.

I found myself with a clan of cantankerous but affectionate old fogies — many of them veterans of the Spanish-American War, the Boer War or World War I. These irascible old-stagers clutched doggedly to the stub ends of their lives, proud of their bigotry, unaware of their impetuous generosity or the fact that old age and habit had turned them into caricatures of their ignorance and equally surprising courage. Old men near death, they would not go down to the ditch meekly. One man struggled for days and when his end approached, he rose up, as if he saw his death, making the walls shake with his shout: "Well, I'll be damned!"

Day by day I saw their old lives wrenched from them and, by contrast, I could feel my youth within me taking up its song of faith in the future, defying the auguries of disaster, singing of tomorrow and the days after. It has not stopped. May it sing in its shroud at my grave.

Every morning, Mr. Duggleby of the Family Aid Committee toured the wards with a Japanese official known variously as Mr. Ohashi, Lieutenant Ohashi or, if one wished to flatter him, Colonel Ohashi. He was, as a matter of fact, a civilian. Handsome and alert, Ohashi moved with a fine bearing and, whenever he caught one's eye, he would give a slight nod and a friendly smile.

On my arrival, Mr. Duggleby told me that my parents were removed to the Remedios Convalescent Hospital in the Malaté district where we had lived with Doña Concepción and her niece, Rosario. Seeing Ohashi had given me an idea: What if I were to ask him to have me transferred to Remedios? I asked the old veterans for advice, but only a minority agreed that I should approach an enemy.

By now I was beginning to get about on my feet again. My legs were still rather shaky, however, and when I tried to climb down the stairs I went tumbling down instead. I had just managed to stand up with the help of the newel post when Mr. Ohashi, accompanied by Mr. Duggleby, came down the stairs. On an impulse, I caught Mr. Ohashi by the sleeve, saying breathlessly, almost swallowing my words, "Please help me. I want to go to Papa and Mama Prising at Remedios."

Ohashi seemed somewhat perplexed, though he pressed my hand warmly, supporting me as he did so. Mr. Duggleby instantly set matters straight by explaining that I had been very ill and that I was the only youngster in Santo Tomás without his parents. He suggested that, when I was strong enough to make the trip, Remedios would be a good place for me to recuperate. To my surprise Ohashi spoke excellent English.

"Very good. I shall do my best for you." And Mr. Ohashi picked me up and carried me to the top of the stairs.

But the days passed by and when Mr. Ohashi made his round of the ward he seemed scarcely to notice me. Mr. Duggleby was afraid nothing could be done about my transfer since the Remedios Hospital might be shut down any day. Nevertheless, he advised me to keep after Ohashi and to pretend that my transfer was a foregone conclusion.

So I tried once more.

Ohashi looked at me frankly and said, "I am sorry. You do not realize that your request is most difficult. I wish to help you but I am not in the position to give the order. Please have patience. And remember that I shall do my best."

The old die-hards had overheard the conversation and snarled and scoffed: Ohashi was teasing me. He was just another two-faced, yellow-pissing Jap like all the rest. I believed in Ohashi, however, trusting him with that quick sense one often has about people.

That very week, the die-hards were absolutely amazed when Mr. Ohashi came straight to my bed with a message.

"Your mother is crying for you. I have seen her and she told me of her many journeys to Japan and of her love for Nikko and Myanoshita. I have told her not to cry and that I wish to make you both happy. She asked me to give you this." Mr. Ohashi handed me a note addressed in Mother's most florid and formal hand:

To my beloved son, Master Robin Prising,
Prisoner of War at Santo Tomás Camp,
By courtesy of the kindly Colonel Ohashi.

I knew at once that Mother had lost none of her gifts. And I could see the curtain slowly falling to the strains of "Hearts and Flowers" in an old melodrama.

On a drizzly morning, after a stormy night, a nurse told me to pack my case. When Mr. Ohashi came on his rounds, he ruffled my hair, saying, "At last I bring good news. Thank you for being patient."

That afternoon, a scraggy horse and carretela (such as were used to take the dead from Santo Tomás) were waiting before the hospital. As Mr. Duggleby wound a white armband round my arm, telling me not to be afraid, I noticed the coachman. He was a very tiny, very old Filipino with eyes that sparked like struck flints in his withered face. He made a strange salute, forming the V for Victory with his fingers while pretending to scratch his forehead. Mr. Duggleby wished me luck and lifted me up into the cart. I found myself sitting beside a prim, supercilious Japanese who wore horn-rimmed glasses and carried a bayonet.

5.

Overhead, clouds blackened the skies; it threatened to rain. The carretela moved precariously past the Main Gate of Santo Tomás, which the sentries flung open and then slammed shut. As we went creaking into Calle España, my guard sat rigidly, his expression utterly contemptuous and, as he doubtless intended I should, I felt small and acutely uncomfortable.

We seemed to be going the wrong way; the horse limped into streets that I did not recognize. Suddenly I had a flash of fear when I saw we were approaching Bilibid prison. Japanese sentries rushed at our cart; they stopped it and jerked me roughly out. The sentries unwound my armband, read the Japanese characters on it and pitched me angrily back into the cart. My guard's face had stiffened into a smirk. When the sentries ordered us to move on, the cochero had to whip the horse violently before it would start. We hobbled through unfamiliar streets until we reached the Avenida Rizal, where I felt a bit easier; at least I knew my way again.

The Filipino cochero whistled merrily as we plodded across the Santa Cruz Bridge, were briefly halted by sentries and ordered to proceed. But the miserable horse refused to move; not even the whip could make it stir. The old coachman had to jump down and lead the horse ahead. When it had started, he climbed back to his seat in front of me.

Bare, desolate Manila, overcast by swollen clouds. No trams, no buses in the streets, only our carretela and truckloads of Japanese soldiers plunging past us. The cochero was whistling again; his tune was unmistakable. I cramped up with panic — would my guard recognize the tune? The guard shifted his bayonet, a smirk fixed to his face. Blithely the coachman continued to whistle "The Star-Spangled Banner."

The carretela lagged along Taft Avenue until it drew into the oval before the Philippine General Hospital. My guard got out and took me up the hospital steps. Officials appeared. Total confusion: arguments in Japanese, in Tagalog, in English. Everyone was talking so fast that the precise little interpreter could not be heard above the din. A Filipino doctor asked me, "Where are your parents? Here, or at Remedios?"

My reply simply increased the altercation.

"Don't worry," the doctor said, bending and shouting into my ear. "Takes time. These Japs don't get anything straight."

At this point, a superbly corpulent Japanese official, in a white uniform festooned with gold medals and braid, made his entrance upon the scene. He had a magnificent white moustache and white, close-cropped hair. With a clap of his hands the official called everyone to order. He came over to me, pinched both my cheeks, chucked my chin, then brought his round, wily face down to mine till our noses touched. Sharp eyes in folds of fat.

"Where do your papa and mama go, baby? Quick-quick! Tell me now!"

"Remedios," I told him.

"Zu-zu-zu!" And he clap-clapped his hands again, dismissing

all but my guard. The official fired questions at the guard. Each reply made the official grow redder and redder and he promptly slapped the guard in the face. Chuckling, the fat official gathered me up and, hugging me close to his medals and braid, he carried me back to the carretela. Whip in hand, the coachman sat in the front seat, grinning at the confusion. Again the Japanese guard took his place beside me, the smirk still fixed to his face.

The cochero clicked and coaxed; he lashed and lashed at the horse until blood ran down in rivulets between its bones. Slowly the wretched animal labored through the empty streets and dragged up to Remedios Convalescent Home. I was safe now.

6.

At Remedios, Father and Mother lived in a narrow wooden hut that housed two other elderly couples. I found them in a makeshift room, partitioned off by piled boxes and a bamboo screen and with the old steamer rug draped over the entrance.

The moment I entered the small, gloomy room my mother gave a heart-tearing cry. She had been fretting about me ever since the Children's Home had shut down. Fortunately she had not learned of my illness until I was recovering at Santa Catalina. Mother had grown old; her skin was sallow and her hair grey. Beauty had left her, though its ghost lingered in the poignant, deep blue eyes. She had lost neither the grace of her movements nor the aristocratic flare of her nose. But she had taken on a genteel, quaint little manner and even her speech had altered. Perhaps it is fortunate that like the chameleon she could change her colors to suit her environment. Mother had abandoned the role of Lovely Lady with its charming air of arrogance and had, almost consciously, assumed a new role in Old Folks' Home.

Worst of all, she seemed childishly secretive. Actually, Mother

was doing much of the smuggling that went on, not only for ourselves, but for other people as well. My first night at Remedios
she took me aside and whispered, "Now you won't tell anyone
anything about us, will you, my pet? Oh, we must be so careful
these days and ever so quiet — just like wee mice." Another time
she called me sternly to her and with a touch of her former
hauteur ordered, "Robin, mark me well: you never see anything; you never hear anything — ever!"

Although I was happy to be with my parents again, I had begun to resent them. When I told them how I had peered
through a window and watched the birth of a baby they considered my enthusiasm ridiculous. I felt that they wanted to protect
me from life as well as death, that they expected me to be the
same child I had been before the war. How could my father sit
out the days by the window, laying the cards for a silly game of
patience; barely able to distinguish a King from a Knave? Who
cared if the cards came out right or not? I was tired of my mother's quaint, secretive air, of being told that I should be a wee,
quiet mouse.

Once every week Mr. Ohashi and Mr. Duggleby made an inspection of Remedios. During the two months since I had arrived, there was a decided change in both men — Mr. Duggleby
looked harried and grim and Mr. Ohashi was aloof, his manner
brusque. Then the order came that by the next fortnight everyone in the hospital would be sent back to Santo Tomás. The
people at Remedios were all old and chronically ill — my mother
was the youngest and strongest in the hospital. I could not imagine most of the patients surviving in Santo Tomás. I was especially worried about old Mrs. Alley, paralyzed and deaf, who had
taught me to talk with her in sign language. Ohashi had helped
me once; I felt certain that, if I asked him, he would have the
order revoked. When I approached him, I broke down and
wept. The remote expression vanished from his face. For a mo-

ment I was terrified of him; his face was contorted with such violent emotion that I thought he was about to strike me. Then his violence flattened suddenly to despondence and turning away from me he said, "I can do nothing more. I do not give orders. I obey them." There was a pause, miserable and embarrassing. Mr. Ohashi withdrew into himself, shamed at having betrayed his feeling before an enemy child.

Mother became very nervous. Strangely, even today, a bewildering shadow of guilt steals over me at the thought of those last days at Remedios. I see my mother before me in our dismal room, her forefinger over her lips, warning me to silence. "Mum's the word. All the walls have ears."

Father Hinehan, Father Lawlor and Father Kelly came to Mother with parcels. I was sent from the room. I heard whispers and unwrapping. In the mornings Mother went round to various inmates distributing small sacks of rice flour, soya beans and mongo beans. They had been sent by Mother's German friend, Lotte. I felt like a criminal when I overheard my parents whisper her name.

The day the Japanese trucks came to take us to Santo Tomás, those who could not walk, like Mrs. Alley, were carried on stretchers. The dying were sent to the Santa Catalina Hospital; others were crammed into the corridors of the Education Building. Mother was assigned to Room Zero on the ground floor of the Main Building. After a week in the Gym, my Father and I were assigned to a room in the centre of the Children's Annex, teeming with fathers and sons.

By night Manila was under blackout and strict curfew. Through the day the Japanese held air-raid drills and air maneuvers and tested their anti-aircraft guns.

The Great Hunger

1.

SANTO TOMÁS had changed for the worse. Two bamboo watch-towers stood at the front and in back of the camp armed by Japanese guards. Lieutenant Colonel Hayashi, commandant of the camp, had a private bunker built for himself directly across from his office. More ominously, sandbag emplacements had been set up at strategic intersections within the grounds. Squads of soldiers prowled about, hatred seething from their eyes: they knew Japan was losing the war.

I had made friends with an older boy in the Annex nicknamed "Russian Harry," who was fluent in English and Russian — he had a remarkable gift of the gab and could make do in French and Dutch as well. Russian Harry kept his ear well cocked for the latest news or rumors and cheerfully passed them along. He knew what the sandbag emplacements were for.

"Machine guns, you boob! When the Yanks come, don't you see, the Nips'll be on the ready to mow us down."

In the hunger lines, in the latrines, in every corridor I heard the same rumor: Every male over ten years old would be shot before a firing squad. The women and the younger children would be shipped to Japan as hostages against the invasion.

This rumor kept getting under my skin. What would happen to my father and me? Since we lived in the Annex, with rooms of women and children on either side of ours, I hoped that we too might be spared. At the same time I could easily imagine my mother being seized with the women and younger children and sent to Japan. Santo Tomás would be half empty then. Father and I would be left in the deserted Annex until the soldiers routed the men and boys from sleep one morning and lined us up before the firing squads.

"Wild horses," Father exclaimed, "couldn't run any faster than that imagination of yours!" and warned me against listening to hearsay as he patiently led me to the sandbag emplacements. They were not gun emplacements, he said, but probably some sort of dugouts in case of air raids. No one else seemed to believe this, nor did the sandbag emplacements look like air-raid shelters to me. I felt that my father was trying to settle my fears, as one did with children.

2.

Father and I were quartered in a large semicircular room in the Annex; a bed-crammed warren of sixty persons, boys under fifteen and their fathers. We were miserably outnumbered by our enemies the bedbugs, some as big as trouser buttons, which infested every mattress and pillow; they bred in our beds, hid in our luggage and entrenched themselves in the seams of our patched mosquito nets. We spent an hour a day picking them out but never got rid of them. I used to take the bugs between my thumb and forefinger, pinch their swollen blisters till they burst, then smell my own blackened blood.

Father's bed was the last one in the room, flat against the wall, so we both had to use the foot of space between us to dress in. Although our corner was suffocating in the heat, we were lucky not to be near the windows, where we would have been drenched by the rains and constantly endangered during the air raids that were soon to come. I did all Father's duties for him: swept beneath both our beds, cleaned the passageways and corridors when our turns came up and washed our clothes. He was too old and ill to do such things himself, but his affectionate, gruffish sense of humor made the tasks go easily as he sat up in his bed, keeping me company and jollying me along. Papa, the one old-stager in the room, was the only man who never lost his temper and never complained. He made a good show keeping our spirits up; his wit was both dry and sweet and his banter prickled with kindness.

The men's latrine, a pit privy with a palm-leaf roof, was a long walk down the corridor and far out beyond the Annex, past a Japanese guardhouse. Father did not use the privy at night but kept an enamel chamber pot, called a po, under his bed. We both had pos before the war, which Alfredo emptied every morning. Now my turn had come. "There goes Prising with his Dad's piss pot," the kids would cry as I went prancing past, nose in the air, bearing the po to the privy.

I woke with a start when the LOUDSPEAKER came blasting on every morning with that same trio of girls (was it the Andrews Sisters?) cutely crooning "Good morning, good morning, we've danced the whole night through . . ." It seemed so crazily sinister, a sarcastic lie. At least the Japanese voices bawling orders at the sentries were a grim fact, an unavoidable reality. Afterwards a cheery American radio voice gave us the rules of our prison camp day as if they were a commercial for a laxative or deodorant. Both the good morning girls and the radio voice were part of the folksy, fake summer camp atmosphere, no doubt intended to boost morale. I wondered why many adults actually enjoyed being treated like children since I despised it so.

Throughout the day I stopped dead every time the LOUDSPEAKER came on. Whose name would be called this time? First the whir of the needle, the recording of a bugle call, then the voice: "Mr. F. W. Prising — Mr. Prising, to the Commandant's Office!"

It was like a slap in the face. People looked at me. Someone advised me to leave the washing in the laundry trough. I hurried over to the front of the Commandant's Office, a small building built like a biscuit box. Father was already inside. Mother had come from Room Zero close by. She was quivering in the effort to mask her terror. Scarcely saying a word, Mother and I paced to and fro. Both of us knew that Father, like many others, was hiding money. The door to the stucco box opened and Papa stepped out. His face was instantly reassuring. "Absolutely nothing," he murmured in that soft, secretive voice we had learned to use. "A routine checkup." He was asked a number of questions: Had he ever been to Japan? How often? Who were his relations in the United States? What was the precise nature of his tobacco business? And then the final question: What do you think of the war?

"The war?" Father smiled gently. "I'll think of *that* when it's over." Commandant Hayashi accepted this reply with a polite chuckle, promptly echoed by his staff, and then Father was dismissed.

3.

By now it was late September, a month almost since we had been brought back to Santo Tomás. At nine in the morning I climbed the three flights of stairs up to lessons on the roof of the Main Building. And each day as I climbed the stairs I could feel my strength draining from me; I was growing weaker. I had not learnt much in the past weeks. It was easier to sit and let my mind drift from my arithmetic, to gaze over the trees in the front grounds, beyond the matted barrier of iron bars and out over the city. The view of church towers, the jumble of streets beneath the corrugated iron roofs of houses and red-tiled roofs of buildings lent me an illusion of freedom as I sat hungry and constrained, muffling some vague feeling of anger. On a fair day I could see as far as the piers and stare at the grey Japanese warships in the bay . . .

The morning was already hot; the iron roofs shone brightly. For many weeks the Japanese had held continual air maneuvers in the Manila skies. Zeros droned and zoomed at each other in mock dogfights, interrupting my view of the city outside. Today, the whole class was distracted by an air duel when we suddenly noticed a smoke puff, then saw one of the Zeros burst into flame. Had the Japanese shot down one of their own planes?

North over Manila a vast white mass of cumulus clouds surged in the sky. There was a dull, indefinite humming in the air and a low vibration. The sound began to grow. And as it swelled into a roar the windowpanes trembled till the concrete building started to shake. Out of the massy surge of clouds, the American bombers came, tier upon tier of them, flying high, flying low, an earth-shaking armada of aeroplanes, glistening silver-white in the sun as they rode the air. Highest of all flew the heavy bombers; just beneath them, dive bombers swerved down towards their targets, with pursuit planes dashing about in escort. As we began to count them, black bombs dropped from their bellies, smashing the harbor and airfields of Manila. While the city quaked beneath the power of planes and exploding bombs we continued counting — thirty, forty-nine, fifty-six, sixty-seven. Sharp anti-aircraft fire broke out; pillars of smoke loomed near the bay; flames lashed taller than bell towers. Only then did the sirens hoot their death warning over Manila. The Japanese had been caught by a surprise attack.

The LOUDSPEAKER switched on: "This is a raid! Take cover!" Machine-gun bullets and shrapnel ripped round as our class on the roof dispersed, stumbling down the stairs and into the Main Building. Throngs of people filled the halls: they kissed; they shouted; they sang. "They're here! They've come back!" Yes, the worst was over: the liberation was at hand; we had no doubt of that. "It won't be long now!" School was suspended. People celebrated by eating up their tinned food. "Why save it? If the Japs could take Manila in a month, the Yanks will do it in half the time!"

Within the next weeks the Japanese turned the stretch of grounds between the Main Building and the Gate into a military supply dump. They pitched tents and billeted soldiers under the trees; they brought in piles of cases and covered them with camouflage tarpaulin. The camp was becoming an arsenal. Was it to hide Japanese supplies from the American planes? Or perhaps part of a plan to massacre us? Russian Harry and I went snooping about to see what we could find. The boxes were filled with machine guns and bullets; the cases were rations for Japanese troops. Commandant Hayashi proclaimed the front grounds out of bounds. The LOUDSPEAKER warned that anyone caught in the vicinity might be shot.

As long as the air raids continued we lived on hopes of early rescue. Then the raids stopped. Days lagged on in famine, with only rumors of invasions to feed us. Everyone passed the rumors along — the Americans had landed in Mindanao; they had established a beachhead at Samar. Every rumor proved false. Russian Harry said that the watchword of the day had become "Cheer up, Johnny, or you'll soon be dead."

By this time we were living on two scant meals a day — breakfast and supper. Those provisions of rice, vegetables and fish that did manage to reach the Main Gate were either worm-infested sweepings or half rotten. Then the good news was announced: we would be given a duck supper. However, the camp ducks, fed on tainted fish and slops, had been dying off and there were only two hundred ducks left, with four thousand prisoners to feed. That Sunday supper of duck: not a shred of meat was visible in the three tablespoons of rice each prisoner received. The ducks had been starving too.

Shortly after this duckless supper, Mother and I encountered a woman whom we recognized as the manageress of the Leonard Wood Hotel. I remembered how Mother had sent her curry back to the kitchen, complaining that it was nothing but gristle and unfit to eat. If the woman had forgotten the incident, to my surprise Mother had not. With touching grace my mother apologized: "I never knew how much we would give for a bit of that gristle today."

4.

Father bought one of the makeshift cook sheds in the East Patio close to Mother's Room Zero. It was a rickety little structure about two yards square with a wooden floor and matted roof of split bamboo. At least it provided a shelter from the rain and sun where Mother could cook whatever she found to supplement the dwindling rations from the camp kitchen. Mother stoked the clay-pot stove with leaves, books, twigs and anything that would burn. She would catch a flame either by holding a magnifying glass over a page in the sun or light a paper from someone else's stove — we had no matches. There was no such thing as a rolling boil. Everything had to be gradually simmered, and it was difficult enough to keep the fire smoldering. A fortnight after the first air raid, our tins of Spam and corned beef were used up, so Mother substituted tins of Pard dog food, which we never actually expected to eat. By late October this too was gone.

We had a meal in famine-stricken November which my father said tasted much like rabbit — a fricassee of pup. Dogs or old tomcats could only be simmered for broth, but puppies were tender. Mother sprinkled the joints of pup with hoarded rice flour, then fried them in the last of our rancid lard. Two cloves of garlic went into the pot to disguise the taste — meat in the tropics quickly starts to turn. When the pup had been browned Mother made a sauce with water thickened with tapioca root, and the fricassee simmered for an hour while we took turns fanning the faltering fire.

That was our biggest feast. Stray pigeons followed. Once we ate part of a cat and in Christmas week the wither from a scavenger dog. There was little meat in these meals, for any stray animals in the camp were down to skin and bones. Poached toad was the one delicacy I could provide, but Mother strictly insisted that toads caught in the latrines must be thoroughly washed.

Even in these days of hunger Mother remained the lady. She never killed a pigeon, a dog or a cat herself but either bartered for or bought it from an enterprising man who had done the dirty work. And she never told us what we were eating until we had finished the meal. Afterwards, a faint, slant smile would flicker over her lips. "I shouldn't like to tell you —" then shrugging the thought away with a queasy little laugh, she would murmur "cat" or "dog."

If it rained or if there were air raids, we ate standing in corridors crowded among other diners. On fine days, however, our irregular meals attempted the formal air. We took our tiffin round a card table propped up outside our cook shed. Before seating herself, Mother primly placed leaves for napkins in front of Father and me. Dressed in an old chiffon tea gown, faded now to the palest coral and grey, Mother gracefully requested the Lord to bless our repast, her tone meekly suggesting that she had done her bit and, if the food was tainted, she expected Him to do His.

Although we ate from old tin cans and without knives, Father insisted upon decorum. "Sit up straight on your box, my boy. I see no reason why your table manners need resemble a baboon's!"

Our silver was what in times gone by we called "the picnic silver": teaspoons and forks with the crests of Raffles Hotel, Singapore, Der Kaiserhof, Berlin, The Cavendish, London, and a consommé spoon from the *Lusitania* — pilfered souvenirs from Mother's many trips. The picnic silver did serve Father's determination that "though we starve on roots and weeds, we shall, by God, preserve some link with a civilized past." Even when

Father's humor began to show signs of strain, I relished these silly formalities; they became our only defiance of circumstances, the relic of our pride.

I bridled sharply, however, if Father tugged at the reins with precepts more genteel. When my thick head of hair and precocious pubic sprouts were nests of nits and lice, he forbade me to use the word "lousy." Nor was I permitted to say "Japs" or "Nips," as the others did. "Call them Japanese," Father admonished. "You will learn, one day, that they are human too."

5.

Lieutenant Abiko was nicknamed "Shitface." My father made me give him my word not to repeat this to Mother, who had never, he assured me, heard such an expression in her life. Of course this pricked my curiosity and when Father was out of earshot I tactfully asked her if she knew what Abiko was called. Mother paused to wrinkle her nose: "I believe he's called Pigface, by some."

Abiko was a petty sadist with a handsomely brutal face. He might have posed for a propaganda poster of the vicious Oriental, and he was the personification of the villain that cinema audiences love to hate. A more sceptical public might have found him unconvincing, for his style was decidedly melodramatic. To us, however, Lieutenant Abiko was both unbelievable and very real. He was the only Japanese at Santo Tomás who was personally despised.

Lieutenant Abiko was a stickler for bowing. It was scandalous, he considered, that we who had been privileged by over two and a half years of Japanese protective custody did not display our gratitude with a deep bow to any passing Japanese — whether officer or petty clerk. Abiko, attended by his interpreter and a squad of soldiers, presided over the roll call at various parts of camp every morning. Once the roll was taken, he drilled us in obeisance. These drills resembled a course in calisthenics since the proper bow was made from the hips — not the waist — the spine kept rigid and the head dropped close to the ground. After a roomful of prisoners performed the bow in unison, he would snigger and grunt with glee. Then, while we stood waiting in humble silence, his mood would shift; Abiko would start to shout, and the entire room would repeat the bow again and again.

Mother had a chance meeting with Lieutenant Abiko near the Commandant's Office. On seeing him, she made a deep and proper bow and he saluted. Without warning Abiko flung himself into one of his barking, stamping tantrums, gesticulating towards his head. Was she expected to salute? She stood at attention and saluted. Abiko's fit simply increased. Meantime a Japanese interpreter stepped briskly to her side and explained:

"In your country, the gentlemen lift their hats to the ladies. You will now overcome your colonialist arrogance by lifting your hat to Nipponese men. You will please to remember that you belong to a third-class people."

For women, there was a special advantage to being a third-class person: they were never raped. But who, I often wondered, were the second-class people — the Filipinos?

Every lad in the Annex was boisterously proud that none of us had ever bowed to a Japanese — except during roll call. Whenever we sighted a Japanese, we retraced our steps and got to our destination by a different route. Once, however, when I was passing the Education Building, Abiko, his sword banging the dust, marched down the road. Pretending I had not noticed him, I cupped my hands over my mouth calling "Harry — ? Harry — !" as if looking for someone. These histrionics neither convinced nor amused Lieutenant Abiko. He planted himself before me, blocking my way. I glanced up at him, acting as if I hadn't the least notion what he expected of me.

Abiko stood motionless. He glared at me with bloodshot eyes, sweat and veins swelling up on his face. There was a hot, drunken smell of saki and sweat. The stamping and shouting started; still I made no move. Abiko raised his boot.

Before I knew it I was sprawling on the ground. He had boxed my ears, dug his boot in my shins and knocked me down. Abiko was yelling and jumping up and down in a slobbering paroxysm of rage. A big pulse of fear went over me: Abiko grabbed for his samurai sword. I kept staring up, so frightened that I felt I had leapt out of my skin.

But then the absurd happened: his sabre simply burst its chain, scabbard and all. Howling, he raised it and began hacking the air. I lay cringing before him, my elbows and knees scraped by gravel. At the same time I was astonished that his sabre had broken the chain and I thought, "How typically Japanese; everything they make always breaks." A deadening blow from his boot came full on my back. Dust and stones flew in my face as Abiko kicked up the earth for good measure; then he grunted and tramped off down the road and out of sight.

I was still shaking as heavily as my heart could pound. Slowly, I pulled myself up; there was a dead, sickly sensation in my back and for a moment I thought I was going to vomit. Suddenly, I was seized by an impulse to run and tell somebody about it — anybody. But I checked myself. If anyone knew that I had bowed to a Japanese, it would shame the record of the other lads in the Annex.

6.

Nearly a month went by before the American planes came back to bomb Manila. When the raids started up again in mid-October, we were strictly forbidden to watch them. Lieutenant Abiko made certain that the rule was enforced as he and his soldiers knocked about the camp trying to catch anyone looking at a plane. If caught, you were slapped and hustled roughly to the guardhouse near the Main Gate, where you were made to stand with folded arms, looking straight ahead, out in the open — despite stray bullets and shrapnel — for a twelve-hour stretch. As the raids persisted, glancing up at the sky at any time might incur such punishment, and some people grew so furtive that whenever they left their rooms they kept their eyes on the ground.

As hunger shrank our bellies, we lived crowded indoors, lying on our beds or sitting in the corridors, for the city was under constant air-alert and the all-clear seldom sounded until dark. Since my room in the Annex had a large half-circle of windows, it was impossible not to see air battles that took place directly in front of them. Until the bombings came too close, every man and boy followed the raids with all the enthusiasm of hooligans at a prizefight. When American pursuit planes grappled with a Japanese Zero, we watched in agonizing suspense. If the Zero broke into flame and smoke, the whole room rioted with applause as it split in half and fell from the air. If an American plane was hit, we silently watched it go into a crazy zoom, zigzagging across the sky; then when it exploded into bits, the room would fill with wretched groans. My father was the only one who never watched a raid. He was posted as a lookout in the corridor, and at his signal that Abiko and his squad were on their way, we scrambled each to the foot of his separate bed, prepared to bow in unison.

During the first raids the Americans showered leaflets over the city, warning the public away from military installations. And, for the most part, the bombing was confined to these targets, though this, of course, meant death for many who lived within their radius. Often the Flying Fortresses bombed from such a high altitude that they missed their objectives and only the neighboring homes were smashed to ruin. I used to watch those impervious B-29's, high in the air, catching the sun in a silvery flare as they flew; and I saw their bombs falling like bird shit over the vague environs of airfields, piers, oil fields and arsenals in Manila. Sometimes in the midst of these raids I began to wonder how much of the city would perish and hoped that our friends outside Santo Tomás would be spared. But I did not think of Terray, my nurse and earliest companion, who lived a fair distance from the oil district of Pandacan. And yet during one of these raids she and her baby were trapped in a cellar, calling and screaming from late afternoon throughout the night. By morning, just when they were on the point of being rescued, the cellar collapsed, crushing Terray and the baby to death.

In Santo Tomás we gaped up at the air raids as if they were a dazzling display of fireworks. Children pointed and cried "flowerbaskets" when the sky was tufted with pretty puffs of pink, green, violet, red and yellow smoke — but the puffs were Japanese tracer shots marking out spaces for anti-aircraft attack. While the air was astounded by battle and the earth went shaking from a fresh storm of bombers raining death on Manila below, starved old grandads looked up and clicked their tongues, their lips parting in smiles of rotten teeth as they croaked, "Yup, lookit our boys up there!"

At midday, as I was watching a dogfight, an American plane began to dribble smoke and the Zero that had sparred with it flew away. The American airman leapt from his stricken plane, and as his chute mushroomed out, machine-gun bullets riddled his body; it jerked, twisted, dangled like a puppet on its strings, then went limp. While the dead body in the parachute slowly descended, the buildings in the camp shuddered against the detonations of blockbusters, flames from an oil fire hurled hundreds of feet high and pursuit planes darted down, strafing at nearby streets. Still the corpse hanging from the strings of the parachute lingered downwards. I froze: suddenly the raid was no longer a spectacular show. I had seen a man killed.

Blood-waves kept rising inside me as the dead man dropped slowly towards earth. My muscle stiffened on my bones in the futile struggle against a feeling that forced itself into thought: "They are under orders." Men in the air and men on the land are under orders to kill. In each plane men are ordered to bomb or strafe; on land the men behind every gun or cannon are ordered to shoot down. But if they broke their orders —? There would be no war. Stop. I became hopelessly confused; logic seemed divided from reason, my thoughts cancelling each other out. Somewhere in the distance the lifeless puppet in the parachute had disappeared.

Curfew was imposed at nightfall; we were under total black-out and the dark hours passed between alert and attack. Sirens went strident through the night; shafts of searchlights crossed each other in the sky, and as I lay in the crowded room of fitful sleepers, the whole room would go bright, the blaze redden and fade on the mosquito nets, men choke and cough from the stench of fires. Hungry, I squirmed and sweated through the hot stress of the night, yearning for food as the rumors of the week went racing through my brain: Americans are landing at Zamboanga; Japanese will take men and boys for slave labor; American beachhead at Batangas; we shall be massacred; an invasion at Legaspi; women and children hostages in Japan; paratroopers will rescue Manila on Christmas Day.

And in those nights, shuttled between sleep and waking, I felt a horrible breaking-down inside me. I felt as though I were only half real, that I was merely a persistent consciousness alert to every shudder of the war that surrounded me, to the misery in the camp and in the city outside. War exploded in the air above me; I heard it in the singing-off of shrapnel and the clatter of bricks close by. In nightmares I could hear it jabbering on radios over Asia and Europe, giving orders to the submarines under the Pacific and Atlantic. War was caught in the eyes of cameras; it moved machines and printed the news of the world.

War haunted me, but I could not grasp it. And I blamed my-self for being a child, for being unable to grasp it.

American paratroopers will invade the city. When the sky blooms with parachutes, machine guns will open fire and we shall see thousands of corpses floating down over Manila. The dead man in the parachute; down, down, so slowly . . . Stirred by the thud of a distant explosion, I imagine a ham sandwich: slices of white bread, pink meat and mustard; then tense to the crack of a close hit, scratch at the bites of bedbugs, claw at my headful of lice. As the room darkens from red, I drowse off with visions of food that turn into nursery rhymes: One potato, two potato, three potato, four potatoes, *more* — Pat-a-cake, pat-a-cake, baker's man, Bake me a cake as fast as you can; Prick it and stick it and mark it with P . . . Says Simple Simon to the pieman, "Let me *taste* your ware" . . . And the corpses of American paratroopers mass themselves and march silently towards our gates; the machine guns are in their emplacements, manned, but Mr. Ohashi is standing by the sandbags struck dumb; he cannot give the order to shoot. Suddenly the room wakes to the blare of the LOUDSPEAKER, the crooning girls and the xylophone; Japanese voices issue orders, American voices issue orders, then the roll call, the sirens, the raids, the rumors and fears of another starving day.

7.

Even as the air rumbled with bombers and the buildings shook with every hit, all of us — men, women and children — copied, exchanged and collected recipes. The craze seized the entire camp. Interrupted only by Japanese search squads or the heaviest explosions, people chattered about supper parties, restaurants, picnics, meals on shipboard, meals with friends and Christmas dinners at home. Uncle John Shaw was past master at such reminiscences. For him haute cuisine had been more than a hobby; it was his prime pursuit. There were long pauses in his recollections by now and he seemed to drift off to the days before World War I, to house parties in Norfolk in the reign of King Edward VII: "We ate green turtle soup and poached turbot . . . eh? — Er, yes; grilled kidney of veal, a haunch of venison — this with black walnut sauce, braised Buckingham duck, a rum omelette, toasted Stilton then, and pears." He would snooze for a bit and waken himself with a snore. ". . . brown sherry, and madeira and port." He made no mention of meals, only feasts.

But I would not be devoured by this obsession with cookery. I escaped into books. My father had given me *Oliver Twist* to read; a fit book, he thought, for a lad going on twelve. In prison camp, however, the story seemed so gruesomely actual that it made me cry bitterly. How could I read about poor Oliver asking for more when my own stomach was eating itself in hunger? I slapped the book shut for the duration, telling myself, "This is bad for your morale."

In the West Patio there was a small room known as the library. Here I took refuge from the raids and the craze for recipes, found the plays of Shakespeare and absorbed myself in *The Merchant of Venice, Othello* and *Hamlet*. In the large, Victorian volumes, I discovered illustrations of famous players so convincing that they seemed to walk out of the pages. I could spend a long afternoon simply gazing at Edwin Booth, stern and dark, as Hamlet; behind his broody, tragic eyes lurked a savagery that could conquer melancholy and spur Hamlet to revenge.

I was consumed by my passion for the theatre, for brave prosceniums and stages that raked sharply up from footlights. I adored old stage sets with their painted backcloths of preposterous castles; I imagined myself among the noisy mobs in the gallery, standing in the pit or leaning forward from the boxes, restlessly awaiting the entrance of the grand tragedian and eager to climb mountains of ecstasy with him.

Most boys of my age dreamt of war, of battles and deeds of derring-do, but for me war was no dream; it was an absolute fact. In our city under daily bombardment, the theatre of my imagination became my brief respite from the reality of war.

When we were brought back to Santo Tomás I had not wanted to escape reality. I hoped to work as a hospital orderly; I wanted to be of use to the sick and dying. If I was old enough to eat from the adult Chow Line, surely I was old enough to be an orderly. My parents merely laughed at this idea, so I went to the hospital and volunteered. But Dr. Stevenson and Dr. Fletcher told me orderlies had to be at least fifteen.

8.

Before starvation took the camp we had waited in the Chow Line with keen, normal appetites and gossiped or bickered with each other, frequently making new friends. Up until the first months of 1944 there was plenty of easy banter in the queues and a good deal of grumbling about the meagre meals. No one ever admitted that the food we had then was the common lot of millions over the world. Like my parents, few of the inmates of Santo Tomás seemed to recognize that they had belonged to a privileged, colonialist class. They saw themselves only as the victims the war had made them, and they considered the war an unjust twist of fate, a mere accident. To me, although I could not have expressed it at the time, our imprisonment seemed a vague, somewhat irrational form of retribution.

Now the famine had come. Twice a day the long, dreary hunger lines formed behind the Main Building. Even the children waited in hungering silence, drooling from their mouths. By this time we squabbled over who came first in the endless queues, and if you left your place for a moment, you were not allowed to reclaim it.

Whenever I think of that great hunger I feel as if I were

gaping into emptiness. In postwar America it was impossible to tell fat, complacent men and women what starvation was like. They simply refused to believe that comfortable, middle-class families exactly like their own could become prisoners of war and patiently starve. When a suburban women's club saw a newsreel of Santo Tomás which flashed by on the screen in a few seconds, they could dismiss their swift glimpses of misery with a squeamish sigh of pity.

The winding queues of wretched prisoners formed hours before a meal was served. And as I waited in the queues from day to day I could watch the other prisoners shrink. Over the first two years of captivity they had lost every ounce of spare fat in an almost invisible process. But now from one day to the next their eyes sank further into their sockets, cheekbones jutted out of paper-thin flesh, knees became gigantic swollen joints attached to the sticks of their legs. The elderly wasted rapidly and, as their slack skin shrivelled and began to crack, they grew into walking corpses. Their staring eyes, once troubled, took on a haunted look; then a milky film crept over cornea and iris — the signal of approaching death.

On hot days, as I joined the waiting queues, the sun seared down at me, as though my skin were meat. Or when it rained, I stood shivering in my bare bones, an absurd figure clad in a frayed shirt, a patched pair of shorts cut from trousers with a rope for a belt. Leaning against the building, I waited in the hunger line with our meal tickets and our pails, tin cans strung with wire handles. Often, just at serving time a raid would start up and the LOUDSPEAKER would order us to take cover until the commandant granted us permission to return. Then I had to find another place as quickly as possible, and keep sharp watch that no one elbow his way before me, or edge in during the later confusion when we moved towards the serving boards.

First the three meal tickets were taken by the kitchen staff and I waited, outwardly patient, while they were inspected for

forgery, the correct date found and each ticket punched —
Father's, Mother's and mine. Then a scoop, made from a can
half the size of a Campbell's soup tin and wired to a stick,
dipped — so very slowly — into a big iron pot. The scoop was
then scraped carefully level and our ration of swill was poured
into the pails. The swill was rotten, soupy rice or rice cooked
with cornmeal, sometimes with bits of meat or greens, but if
these slightly savored the saltless slop, they could not be seen.
The boiled white worms and tiny stones, however, were easy
to see.

If a drop of gruel or a grain of soggy rice dribbled to the rough-
hewn wooden table, I stretched out a finger to wipe it up, but if
I reached for anything that spilt to the ground, the person behind me would stay my hand, warning me against dysentery.
At last, a generous dipper of tea, coffee or ginger water, with flies
and bugs afloat in it, filled up my largest pail.

On rare occasions, Sundays or the Mikado's birthday, a small
thumb of banana or perhaps a quarter-cup of coconut milk or
the liquid waste from soybean cattle feed might be included
with our fare. These were so delicious that the mere taste of
them hurt.

9.

A sallow youth of fifteen with round, old-fashioned glasses
wandered about Santo Tomás, stooping slightly as if he carried
a pack on his back. People spoke of him in whispers. He was
brought into the camp from Fort Santiago, where he had been
severely cross-examined by the Japanese military police. Ulti-
mately the Japanese had pronounced him innocent, then,
merely forgetting about him, left the lad to rot in the fort for five
months. The whisperers said that he had seen his mother tor-
tured to death, that he had spent his time in solitary confinement and that when he was brought to Santo Tomás the Japa-

nese told him he would be shot if he mentioned his experiences in the torture house. But the stories about his mother differed. Some said she had worked with the guerrillas; other believed she had smuggled diphtheria antitoxin up to the Death March survivors in the military prison camp at Cabanatuan. I never knew the facts.

My parents, frightened lest they be implicated in his mother's activities, forbade me to be seen in his company. One never knew who might be listening: there were spies in Santo Tomás, hungry informers who distorted the most trivial conversation and were paid by the Japanese in bean curd or a piece of fish.

I disregarded my parents' order; their attitude seemed cowardly and shameful and only served to charge the air around our slight friendship with secrecy. Besides, I felt that I had something in common with the lad: until I found old Ma Sanders, I too had been alone in Santo Tomás, although my circumstances were far less miserable than his. I had grown fond of this boy with an unusually intelligent face and natural, quiet manner. And I wanted to be his friend. But I knew it was his nature to carry his pack in silence. If I had asked him questions he would have found them an intrusion, an invasion of privacy. And in Santo Tomás the privacy of one's thoughts was all one had left. As a sign in a latrine said: IF YOU WANT PRIVACY CLOSE YOUR EYES.

Gradually an understanding grew between us. Whenever I saw my friend coming towards the hunger line, I took my place behind him, as if by accident, so he would be served first. And as he met my glance, his step quickened and a smile would shy over his face. We were both starving. He, however, had no mother to cook him wild colitus and pigweed stews twice a week; his meals came from the Chow Line alone.

My mother had traded a gold keepsake bracelet for a block of chocolate. Each square of this chocolate was supposed to have sufficient nourishment for one day. While it lasted, she gave me a precious square twice a week, on the days when we did not have a stew. I refused to eat the chocolate in front of her, saying that I preferred to save it until I went to bed at night.

Then I took that square of chocolate and kept smelling it, going crazy from its rich, powerful odor; sometimes I could not resist the temptation to lick it. And I would seek out my friend, tell him that Mother gave me a piece every day and that I did not need it. He refused when I first offered it, but if he was difficult to persuade, hunger forced him to relent in the end.

Today the odor of dark, bittersweet chocolate brings him to mind. We have not met since 1945, but when the image of his face moves towards me, I remember our friendship in that time of famine and remember his uprooted youth. I should be happier today if I knew that, when he became a man, he found reason to be glad.

10.

As famine increased, various labor details were laid off work until only the kitchen, vegetable garden and hospital workers remained. It was the heavy labor squad that chopped the wood, built the fires, shouldered huge sacks and stirred the steaming cauldrons of our gruel. These volunteers, the camp's strongest men, lived on the same scant ration as the rest of us. Several kitchen details had been dismissed for stealing food. But who could blame them? For by their toil the camp survived.

Before curfew every evening, on my way to the Annex, I pass the camp kitchen sheds and see the men laboring over the square cement kilns in which the big, round cauldrons lie. In the half-light, four men stand on the corners of each kiln holding long, wooden oars in their hands; slowly, rhythmically they dip their oars into the cauldrons and stir. Stripped to the waist, the men are clad in shorts and wooden clogs; their voices, groans echo around me. Almost subhuman in this infernal dusk, they drudge over tomorrow's breakfast as if, like Sisyphus or Tantalus, they were condemned to futile struggle in the underworld. And these stark figures, whose arms and legs look like rough ropes knotted at their joints, are emaciated men; their thews have wasted on their bones. In this slow dusk they stand on top of the fiery kilns, tantalized by vats of the gruel which they must cook. Staggering from hunger and the heat, the men go faint over their task and, one by one, each takes his turn to pause, wiping the sweat from face and armpits, while the others stand unsteadily, continuously stirring the cauldrons of boiling cornmeal, worms and stones.

11.

Bright day. As I step out of the cool, unreal world of the library, deserted cook sheds tilt uncertainly at me. I blink at them, trying to put them and the afternoon into focus. Mind where you are going: Japanese soldiers are posted at the exits of the building. Is it a search? I shall have to bow to them if I leave the building. Turn the other way. Nervous women chatter and flutter past me as I head off towards Room Zero. Mother is coming towards me down the corridor, her eyes dilated, a warning finger placed over her lips.

The Kempe Tai have arrested four men: Carroll Calkins Grinnell, chief of the Internee Committee, my friend Mr. Duggleby of the Family Aid, and two others, Johnson and Larsen, neither of whom is a camp official. Agatha Cook tells us that three of them are locked up in the detention room just off the main hall. Mother keeps repeating, "Such a pity. Such a pity!" while other women are buzzing about us like furtive flies.

"Larsen's a case of mistaken identity."

"Grinnel and Duggleby could be suspected of anything."

"Yes, anything — smuggling food?"

"Contact with guerrillas?"

"Hiding a radio?"

"What about Johnson?"

"Took him out of camp, they did."

"Everybody knows Johnson. Johnson *talks too much.*"

Meanwhile Grinnell's shanty and Duggleby's office have been raked with a fine-toothed Japanese comb, their papers ransacked and confiscated. Presently a search squad of soldiers is on its way to Room Zero. Mother hastens me off.

"Be a good lad and bow to the soldiers and go back to your father in the Annex, my pet."

That evening at roll call, as we stand at the foot of our beds, my father remarks out of the corner of his mouth, prisoner fashion:

"Couldn't you find a better hide-out for that camera? Anyone can see it in the men's latrine."

After lights-out I lie racking my brain for a safer hiding place and suddenly remember a hole in an acacia tree. Next morning, between roll call and breakfast, I put the camera in the hole, concealing it with a clump of leaves. And just in time too.

When Lieutenant Abiko and his men come tramping into our room for inspection, all contraband is safely stowed, our luggage at the foot of our beds. We stand at the foot of our beds and bow. They bow. We smile, they smile. Whereupon, to our surprise, they leave. Today is Christmas Eve.

May men learn to live contentedly.
Merry Christmas and a Happy New Year
at least happier than this one
to Mama
from
Robin
May the little Christ Child look upon our
needs this year.

Christmas 1944: a day like any other. I gave my mother my best sketches of air raids made on flyleaves torn from books. The sketch of which I was proudest showed the American airman bailing out in his parachute while machine-gun fire from the ground filled him with shot. But I felt something was wrong, that my drawings might not be proper Christmas gifts. So I scrawled the preceding message on an old picture card of the town of Bethlehem.

Father and I exchanged more practical presents. He gave me a toothbrush and some pencil stubs; I had made him a pair of shoestrings from twine carefully blackened with crayon. On this, their thirty-second Christmas together, Father had only the gift of praise and a kiss for his loving wife, from whom he received a half-dozen handkerchiefs of varying sizes — remnants from bed sheets, hemmed by her hand. My Christmas box from Mother was more than a token; it was precious as myrrh and frankincense but more useful. A cake of Cashmere Bouquet soap.

Close to a year had passed since I had bathed with soap and then only the scentless, nunnery soap of the Children's Home. At first I wanted to eat it and bit greedily into it, but since the soap proved inedible I brushed my teeth with it instead. Then I took the Cashmere Bouquet to the shower. As I scrubbed myself down, working up a rich lather over my skin and bones, the shower room became suffused with a cloying fragrance.

"Holy smoke! What's that?"

"Sure smells like Merry Christmas to me!"

I passed the soap round; thin hands grasped it as if it were treasure and everyone lathered from head to toe. We smelt of it for days. When we stood in the Chow Line, the malodorous mob, reeking of sour sweat and prison camp, went jealously sniffing and sniggering at us.

"What's the matter with you, boy?" asked a shirtless, shrivelled Blimp, still sporting his pith helmet and moustache. "You smell like a servant gal back from a fair!"

Hope is strong meat for the hungry and there had been a rumor of a Christmas truce — as in World War I. Hundreds of American planes were expected to fly over the camp, para-

chuting parcels of food. At daybreak on Christmas, a squadron
of American planes did fly low over Manila. There were no
parachutes of food, but the planes scattered leaflets: WISHING
THE PEOPLE OF THE PHILIPPINES THE BLESSINGS OF CHRISTMAS AND
THE REALIZATION OF THEIR FERVENT HOPES FOR THE NEW YEAR.
This, we felt certain, promised freedom by New Year's Day.

Those families that could, celebrated with a Christmas dinner
of cat or dog or bird. Knowing that an extra serving of rice
would be ladled from the Chow Line, Mother decided not to
cook that day. Like everyone else, we received a spoonful of
jam. I saved mine for two days, then greedily gobbled it. The
jam, strong as Napoleon brandy, sent flames of temporary energy
through my veins until my head went winged and wild with
hopes. I was drunk from the sugar.

Starvation is taking its slow toll. Seeds of fear are sprouting
quickly now: We know that we are near the beginning of the
end — will the end be massacre or liberation? In the last week
of 1944 I discover that I can no longer run; that whenever I begin to hurry my knees knock together and my legs sag under
the weight of my fragile body. I can count my bones from the
collarbone down — each joint, each jutting rib. Waiting under
the hot sun in the hunger lines, I break into cold sweats. Unable
to keep my knees straight, I grow faint, struggling against the
terror that I may black out and spill the food on the ground.

The slop is more wormy and watery now and almost tasteless.
By New Year's Day I have developed a habit of vomiting up,
and swallowing again, a mouthful of food for an hour or so
after the two scoops of gruel each day. Even the vomit tastes
good. I go to the latrine as seldom as possible, trying to hold
everything inside me, stingily preserving it for two or three days.
And without any pity, but in cold disgust, I notice that many
prisoners are losing their minds and furtively devour imaginary
meals, slurping and eating the air. Men suck their thumbs,
gnaw at their hands.

My parents have grown gaunt and ugly, mere ghosts of their former selves. Mother is so thin that her eyes and ears are enormous, the flesh of her arms hangs on her bones like a sleeve, her hands are knucklebone. Father's beard has stopped growing; he has no need to shave, not twice a week, and he no longer bothers to sharpen old razor blades. After roll call, when he undresses, I can see how his skin drips on his skeleton; the cavities are deep at his thighs and buttocks. Only his hands, his ankles and his feet are fattening — swollen from beriberi. Father's eyes are growing a milky film; from day to day he becomes more quiet, more abstracted and gentler than ever. As he lies on his bed, unless his breathing is labored, I have to glance over at him to make certain he is still alive. If he notices me looking at him, he can scarcely smile.

12.

Today, the sixth of January, fires from American bombs smolder in the city. Three years have gone by since the Japanese soldiers jumped out of cattle vans and arrested us at bayonet point. The Americans have not landed on our island of Luzon, nor is there any sign of a Japanese retreat. It is merely a question of survival now: If the Japanese do not gun us down, an epidemic of dysentery, cholera or typhoid would fill our beds with corpses.

Grinnell, Duggleby and Larsen were taken from camp thirt-teen days after being locked in the detention room. None of us saw the men again.

But their corpses were found. After the Americans captured Manila, search parties tracked down every clue until they discovered a heap of rotting, dismembered remains. The men had been beheaded and their bodies were gruesomely wired together with fourteen others. The severed heads and trunks were in such wretched decay that the men could be identified only by bits of their clothing, by the fillings in their teeth and Grinnell's broken glasses. The truncated corpses were discovered in a wasteland of marsh and rank overgrowth near Fort Antonio de Abad, the crumbling remains of the Spanish-American War, just beyond the street where we lived under house arrest.

The month of January is prolonged into a timeless drifting within those pallid grey precincts of limbo, which had so terrified me in catechism class. Days pass over like the shadows of bombers cast on the ground by the sun; all color is gone, all sense of being, lost in a progression of negatives. And each grey dawn wakes us to the sound of sirens, the falling of bombs, and we wait in hunger and heat, beset by the fear of massacre. Suspended in that precarious state between waking and sleep I dangle in a recurrent dream: Americans break into the camp; the Japanese turn their machine-gun fire in every direction; all I need do is to run but my legs give way beneath me.

"The Americans have landed on Luzon." The news goes down the breakfast queue; everyone is astir; I waken as I stand there waiting. "They have established a beachhead at the Lingayen Gulf, two hundred kilometres from Manila." My shy, sad friend of fifteen joins me. I pass the word to him. He nods, telling me that the Japanese in camp spent the night packing their gear and burning their records. Later in the morning we watch a chaotic file of Japanese soldiers, their kits strapped to their backs, pushing off from the camp on bicycles.

Next day Mr. Lloyd and Mr. Carroll, representatives of British and American prisoners, are held hostage with their interpreters in the Commandant's Office while Lieutenant Colonel Hayashi and his staff prepare to abandon the camp. Eight hours later the hostages are released. At roll call the LOUDSPEAKER announces that Commandant Hayashi has altered his plans: he will remain.

The entire morning of January seventeenth is spent in roll call. We stand famished and exhausted while the whole camp is counted, recounted and counted again. Last night a man called Eisenberg escaped. The Japanese threaten to inflict severe punishment on the Internee Committee, the room monitors and the rest of the prisoners. But their threats are plainly bombast. I keep wondering how Eisenberg had the physical strength to escape when I could not even manage to run.

At one time a hearse motored hurriedly into Santo Tomás to spirit off the dead. But in these days a carretela with its haggard horse and silent coachman turns slowly past the Main Gate, bearing our dead of the day. With its cartwheels creaking and the horse's hoofs drumming the dry dirt, it carries the bodies of friends and acquaintances, some of whom I knew in the Gymnasium, Remedios or Santa Catalina Hospital, some of whom I had met in the hunger lines and others I knew only by name or sight.

Old Uncle John Shaw died on a Sunday morning, a soft and silent morning before the heat of the sun. No horse and carriage came through the gate for him. Two young Filipino lads wheeled a pushcart into Santo Tomás. I watched them lift a makeshift plywood coffin, scarcely brushed with whitewash, onto the cart. And as they rattled him off, I remembered the grand old gentleman in his suite of rooms at the Manila Hotel, Aunt Jessie, his wife, who had died before the war, and their pugnacious green parrot that loved to peck at me. Uncle John was the head of the Canadian Pacific Steamship Company in Manila — he booked all our trips in the *Empress of Japan*. The coffin was joggling lightly and easily on the cart, as though it were empty. Uncle John Shaw, the magnificent gourmet, lost over a hundred and fifty pounds as a prisoner of war. The fattest man I have ever known died of starvation.

13.

Manila is overhung with a pall of black smoke. The air is heavy from the burning and for years afterwards the acrid smell of smoke will stifle me, bringing back the stench of the war, with its load of hunger and death. Imperceptibly the causes of these fires have changed. No longer started by American bombs and guerrilla sabotage alone, they are now being set by the Imperial Japanese Army in preparation for the Battle of Manila. Along with the noises of heavy bombardments we hear the arsenals exploding and from some great distance the report of artillery fire. From neighborhoods outside Santo Tomás comes a rising din of howling dogs, shouts, strange cries of birds; intermittently throughout the night the startled cocks are crowing, sentinels of a troubled countryside.

By the last week in January many prisoners are so weakened and wasted that even immediate relief will not save them. Dr. Stevenson, chief of the medical staff, has refused to strike the words "malnutrition" and "starvation" from the death certificates. The Japanese insist that the increasing number of deaths is merely caused by heart failure. Angered by his protest, the commandant has locked Dr. Stevenson in the camp jail. Will he vanish from Santo Tomás too, like Mr. Duggleby and Mr. Grinnell?

The thirty-one days of January have worn slowly by, days of rat soup and weeds. Although the Japanese remain our masters, the flashes of artillery fire by night signal the American advance. From the hills to the north, distant and remote, the artillery fire begins, stops and then begins again. In our prison camp, we keep eyeing the sandbag emplacements in terror lest in some desperate and final act the Japanese train their guns on us.

In the anguish of waiting, freedom appears like some grotesque mirage. Through the slow procession of days, through the famine and the dread, the camp has kept up a spirit of gritty optimism which blindly — sometimes absurdly — shuns despair. The prisoners in Santo Tomás have become one in adversity, sharing the same hope, the same courage. Starvation has sapped our bodies, it has exposed our skeletons beneath the residue of flesh and veins, but it has refined our understanding. An ineffable patience pervades this tragic commonalty: patience with the impatience of others. We have become part of the living, the dying and the dead. We are merged into the single indomitable will to endure. Though our eyes glister from hunger, flesh shrinks, knees buckle and individual lives break down to death, we shall survive. And in the harsh triumph of pity and terror, I sense the rhythm and surge of humanity, life and death abiding in chaos within each one of us.

We are still waiting. We are always hungry.

I V

World Without End

Manila, Goodbye

1.

THE PASIG RIVER cuts through Manila, dividing my life and the city in half. Santo Tomás lies north of the Pasig, close to the city outskirts. By the first of February the American Army began closing down on Manila from the north and south. At San Fernando, some sixty kilometres to the north, the 1st Cavalry sent a flying column, backed by tanks from its 44th Battalion, through the Japanese lines and towards the city. Their primary objective was to take Santo Tomás and rescue the four thousand Allied prisoners of war.

Just before sundown on Saturday, February third, Captain Manuel Colayco of the Guerrilla Intelligence Unit was waiting in the northernmost suburbs of the city to make contact with the American brigade. Somewhere far south of Manila he could hear the distant gunfire of American artillery, but from the north he could actually feel the earth shake under the weight of the approaching army.

The sun had set. Manila glowed dull red from the fires of Japanese demolitions and American bombings. In the red light of this unsettled darkness the first tank appeared. Captain Colayco jumped into a jeep that headed the column of tanks, field guns, rocket launchers and a thousand men. Familiar with the tank traps and land mines set in the streets of Manila, the Filipino captain would guide the American troops to Santo Tomás.

At seven o'clock they reached the city limits, to be greeted by firing from the Cemeterio del Norte, where my father now lies buried. Unharmed, the column pushed into the city, moving swiftly at first, then cautiously, as Captain Colayco guided it through the web of mined streets which he knew so well. Proceeding with neither mishap nor incident, they evaded the death traps that had been laid to impede the inevitable American invasion.

Santo Tomás lay in blackout, a vast enclosed compound in the centre of which stood the sombre outline of the Main Building with its tower topped by a cross. As they approached the matted fence, a task force of a hundred men broke ranks to scale the iron spearheads and take the Japanese guards from behind. Still guided by Captain Colayco, the five tanks at his side turned and faced the Main Gate of Santo Tomás. It was almost nine o'clock. Shots burst from within the camp. The tanks crashed through the Gate, moving heavily ahead. Quickly, the jeep thrust past the Gate, driving alongside the tanks. A grenade tossed from the Japanese guardhouse exploded in the jeep. Captain Manuel Colayco was dead.

2.

Early that same day of February third, the prisoners in Santo Tomás had no premonition of these events. The Rising Sun still flew from the flagstaff before the Main Building. Hunger was more immediate and the fear of a massacre was spreading, for the Japanese had demanded a list of every able-bodied male between the ages of eighteen and fifty. Would the rest of us be killed while the men were taken for slave labor?

Twice, today, I have stood limp and empty waiting in the hunger line. The shoelaces I made for my father at Christmas are useless. Beriberi has blown up his feet as big as balloons so that he can barely get into his shoes. Next week the shoes may have to be cut.

In the late afternoon, I kiss my mother good night at Room Zero and cross past our cook shed. Suddenly a brisk droning and as I glance up over the patio palms half a dozen American planes buzz past, dipping so low that they fairly graze the building. Everyone in the patio bursts into applause and cheering. I had seen a pilot smiling.

A snap within me. My head goes giddy; a fresh energy thrills in my blood. I try to hurry back to my mother, as fast as my buckling knees will let me. The hallway outside her room is alert with people: in three years no one has seen American aircraft fly so close. I have almost forgotten my hunger.

"Not bombers," I tell my mother, "pursuit planes — P-38's. One of the pilots smiled!"

Voices break into each other, everyone talking at once.

"The Japs didn't even fire at them!"

"Must have made an agreement to surrender the city."

"What did Mr. Leary say?"

"Going to strafe a battalion of Jap tanks coming this way."

A woman stumbles in from the patio, giggling and faint. She holds a bit of paper in her hands.

"I copied it! See, one of them planes dropped some kind of goggles. Look at this — the pilot went and wrapped a note to them. It says 'ROLL OUT THE BARREL'!"

Warning me not to become too excited, Mother kisses me good night again and sends me to my father in the Annex. Curfew is an hour away.

Reeling out of the Main Building I pass the heavy labor squad, hard at its task over the cauldrons of gruel. When I reach the Annex corridor I nearly collide with Mrs. Seater. Our brains as usual work in the same direction: we are certain that the Americans will take the camp by morning.

Mrs. Seater has been my one bright light through these dismal days. "A divorcée," my mother once told me, her voice edged with slight disapproval. I've no idea whether she was one, but nothing could have attracted me to Mrs. Seater more except the stares she receives for wearing scuffed silver evening slippers with precariously high heels. She prefers them, quite sensibly, to going barefoot. Before coming out to the tropics, Mrs. Seater lived in Alaska which, at least to me, lends her the atmosphere of an adventuress. Her hair is sun-bleached and her dresses, the last word in Santo Tomás elegance, have the has-been air. Mrs. Seater has three small tins of food in her suitcase. She opens the tin which has lost its label, and it turns out to be beef stew. She gives her daughter Daphne a mouthful, then gives me one, and takes a spoonful herself till we finish the tin. It is a celebration.

The stew makes me dizzy as a merry-go-round, so much salt and flavor that I begin to feel sick. What a terrible thing it would be to puke such a good stew. Happily, whirling in nausea, I set out to find my father.

At sunset, on our last day under the Rising Sun, my father is sitting quietly on the porch at the side entrance to the Annex. The sky is streaked with clouds that look like streamers of blood-soaked bandages; smoke and the smell of burning linger in the air. At the time of the setting sun, Father sits on the Annex porch just as he always sat on the verandah at home — only he has no cigar, no seeds for Napoleon, no newspaper, no whisky. He sits there calmly accepting the sundown, which today, as if on purpose, is a magnificent burning.

"They'll be here by dawn!" I announce melodramatically, creeping up from behind.

Father sits motionless, shrunk from famine; the tongues of his shoes are splayed open by big beriberi feet. His voice is weak and resigned.

"No, not tomorrow. Tomorrow is Sunday. They wouldn't come on a Sunday."

Sobering slightly, I sit beside him and watch the gory blaze of the setting sun, convinced that it is a portent in the sky which he refuses to recognize. A sunset to Father is a sunset, just as it has always been. I remember how in 1940 I sat with my father on the verandah of our home by the sea. "There's going to be a war," I had said. "No, there won't be a war," he replied comfortably, but with emphasis.

Everything is disturbed: birds shriek, fires burn in the city, the earth is shuddering. From the distance a massive pressure seems to be pushing towards us. It comes from the north, inexorably as the sundown in the west and the curfew that must follow. The sun is dropping fast. The shuddering in the earth grows heavier and heavier; soon it is interspersed by the rapid rattle of machine-gun fire. A grinding roar mounts heavily and, as the staccato reports of firing increase, night hoods the dull red city. Flares break out from the suburbs in the north.

The LOUDSPEAKER blasts from every tree and building in the camp: "All internees, all internees, go inside the buildings. Keep away from windows."

Slowly Father rises from his seat. "Well, I guess it's time to turn in." He says it so simply, as any old gentleman does when the sun drops down and the evening damp drives him in.

"I want to watch!"

"You'll do nothing of the kind." His voice is a bit firmer now. "Nearly time for roll call. Time for bed." Father takes a heavy breath, coughs, then a trace of humor wavers in his tone. "If you stay out here somebody or other'll be after you with a Gatling gun." I begin to wonder if "Gatling gun" is an expression from the Spanish-American War, or maybe from World War I.

My father is the oldest man in the Annex.

3.

Shortly after roll call the electrical current failed. The lights went off. The LOUDSPEAKER was dead. In our dark dormitory someone cries, "Guerrilla sabotage!"

Father has climbed wearily under his mosquito net and into bed. Presently he falls asleep, his head supported by three fusty pillows. Inside my mosquito net I lie listening in the rumbling blackout. The bedbugs have come out for supper. Turning, twisting, scratching I can hear the whole night roar. Machine-gun fire, the reply of rifle shots. Hunger. I vomit back a mouthful of stew. Go dizzy. The suspense tightens over me; the bedbugs are filling their bags with my blood. Rustling in the room, then boys' voices out in the corridor piping excitedly through the din and darkness. I slip from my bed and grope my way into the corridor. I can just make out the hatchet of Russian Harry's profile, edged with a shock of flaxen hair.

"Who's coming with me?" asks Russian Harry. Alastair volunteers. And the two lads go out to reconnoitre. The rest of us wait with weak, wobbling knees; our hearts pulse to the reverberating roar. Suddenly light comes bursting through the window, the entire camp goes bright, then a crack of shots from close by. The dark comes down again; everyone in the Annex is awake. Babies crying, voices calling out. The foundations of the building quake under the noise of treading tractors.

"Mummy — ! Mummy!" The cries of a frightened child. Then the cross reply of a mother, "Oh Mandy, do shut up!"

A cold hand clutches my arm in the dark. I am so scared that my voice sticks in my throat. It is Russian Harry. He goes jabbering on about how he and Alastair sneaked round the back of the Main Building. A man told them that a truckload of Japanese soldiers, which had left before sundown, had returned to the Education Building an hour ago.

Massive shouts, huge yells, repeat and repeat in the blackout. The shouts come in tidal waves, like the cheering mobs at a football game. "RAY — RAY-EEE! HOO-RAY-EEE!"

The shouts pulled us towards them. Already we were out of the Annex, slipping past the kitchen sheds in the dim starlight, hugging the shadows, creeping under cover of darkness through

Eight years old, a month before the war.

With Father and the "mongrel pup."

Mother in her theatre days.

The Empress of Japan.

With Ah Yee, my Chinese amah.

F. W. Prising: Tobacco Products.

"Mr. Prising's car."

Confiscated Japanese photo.

The Main Building, Santo Tomás.

Prisoners of war arriving.

Confiscated Japanese photo.

THE LITTLE TOWN OF BETHLEHEM

LOOKING WEST FROM THE BELFRY OF THE GREEK
TOWER OF THE CHURCH OF THE NATIVITY. BETHLEHEM
IS ALMOST ENTIRELY A CHRISTIAN TOWN. HOWEVER, A
MINARET OF A MOHAMMEDAN MOSQUE CAN BE SEEN AT
THE UPPER END OF MANGER SQUARE.

With best wishes

For a Merry Christmas

And a Happy New Year

Christmas card 1944.

Merry Christmas and a
Happy New Year —
at least happier than this one
to Mama
from
Robin
May the little Christ child look upon
ur needs this year..
Christmas 1944.

Arnold Genthe photo, courtesy of Miss Eva Le Gallienne.

Eleonora Duse.

Pasadena Star-News.

Mrs. Mildred Brown Sanders, 1948.

Survivors: Lee Rogers and John C. Todd,
old friends of my father's.

Santo Tomás gymnasium.

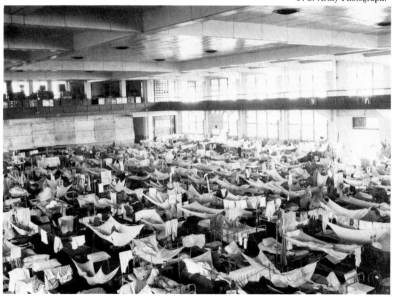

U. S. Office of War Information (National Archives).

American guns at Santo Tomás during the Battle for Manila.

Manila begins to rebuild.

Bert Brandt — Acme photo, courtesy of Compix.

the sightless realms. The shouting continued. We tried to hurry. We were so scared, so weak, so belly-cramped that our knees sagged. At last we groped our way into the back entrance of the Main Building. We bumped into each other, stumbled, were caught by other weak, jittery people, then linked hands and made our way into the patio.

The beam from a powerful headlight cuts into the patio, knifing our eyes. It comes from the main entrance, illuminating swarms of wraithlike people in the hall. Laughter, cheers and the weeping of women. "They're here! They *are* here!" Our eyes grow accustomed to the light that floods from a tank at the entrance way. A jumble of people on the stairs, photographers flash their lights, bulbs pop . . .

But then my bones stiffen at the joints, my gut hardens and my teeth set tight. Who are these men? They are tall, they are jaundice-yellow, they are wearing NAZI helmets. Are they German soldiers come to help the Japanese? In the assault of the headlights these well-fleshed, queerly yellow-tan men are clustered round the women who keep hugging them. Old men pluck at the sleeves of their battle dress, thumping on the invaders' backs. The soldiers break into great white smiles with teeth that look like gravestones.

Two enormous, warm, square hands catch me round the waist lifting me high above the crowds and onto gigantic shoulders.

"Want to see what's going on, sonny?"

The violence of light, the press of the crowd swimming under me and my eyes fill from the glare, from six months' strain and starvation, from the warmth of those so healthy hands and this blue-eyed Yank laughing up at me, a stranger turned new friend in the night.

He sets me down, but I will not let go of his hand. I want to take him, like some incredible human present, to show to my mother. When we find her in the thronged passage near Room Zero, she stares up at the tall young soldier, her eyes brighter than gold-flecked lapis in her hunger-shrivelled face. Then with a sudden gesture, she raises her hands high to his face, her head thrust back in triumph. But her voice locks in her throat and when she does speak, the words break with difficulty:

"Is it all — over, then?"

4.

On my way back to the Annex with a flashlight the Yank has given me, a mob drags me towards the women's lavatory. Crude shouts rage from the mob; profanity pours out of a woman who never seems to pause for breath. The mob surges backwards and forwards, catching me into its net, drawing me closer to a small room next to the lavatory.

"Kick him for me!"

"Here, take that, you bastard!"

"Shitface, you fucking swine!"

Groaning issues out of the hollow room and, pressed closer, I see a Japanese soldier writhing on the floor. Lieutenant Abiko has been shot in the belly. One of his ears is slashed half off; a woman pokes the burning butt of an American cigarette in his face.

"Don't kill him yet; give him a kick!"

"Let me get at him; I'll give it to him!"

"Fat, filthy, yellow-bellied Jap!"

"I ain't ever gonna bow to you again, Shitface!"

Abiko howls and struggles, his body wracked by sudden jolts; a man bends over him, slitting off his buttons for souvenirs.

"These are sure gonna cost somethin' some day!"

Drenched in thick blood, Abiko thrashes there, half dead. Animal noises and jerks are all that is left of him. The timid or the squeamish simply spit on him while he wriggles in their spit and his own blood, stinking of urine. A few, like myself, stand watching, confused by revulsion and guilt. The guilt is for the pity. In wartime your ration of tears must be shed in the appropriate place, your pity reserved for your own wounded and dying. Not for the enemy. This morning or this afternoon it might have been one of us who lay shot and squirming. But tonight it is Abiko. And as the Japanese officer sprawls on the cement floor, blood frothing from his mouth, his legs encased in military boots, the gargling rasps that come from his throat are softer than the curses of those who were once his prisoners. For my own part I am revolted by the sight of him thrashing there and by the rabble spewing abuse at this dying animal. At the same time I feel partly aloof from the zone of his dying, although I keep watching because death, like birth, is something boys of my age rarely see. Later I shall boast of having watched, but it will be years before I admit to the pity that lurks in my disgust — then I shall brag about that too.

After I left the room, I found my father waiting for me in the dark Annex corridor. With the Yank's flashlight I was able to take him over to my mother. On our way through the Main Building, I offered to show him Abiko, whose groans could still be heard beneath the rabble's curses. Father had no interest in him whatever. When word came that Abiko was dead, Mother remarked, "Dead? Then that's best for him."

Mr. Ohashi and two other Japanese had surrendered their samurai swords and become prisoners of the Americans. I was a bit uneasy thinking about Mr. Ohashi. For the wind of vengeance was up now that Commandant Hayashi was holding over two hundred men and boys hostage in the Education Building. He had remained there with a hundred Japanese soldiers, refusing to leave the building.

As the night wore on, most of the camp smoked GI cigarettes and celebrated in song while American sharpshooters ringed the Education Building and Mr. Stanley, the British interpreter, was calling up to the Japanese trying to arrange terms. At one point the Japanese shot their rifles from the windows; an American tank turned on its headlights and opened fire. Inside the building, hostages cowered under their beds with the Japanese for company.

Father ordered me back to the Annex and to bed, where I lay, unable to sleep, with a chaos of images racing through my mind. How strange the American invaders looked. They were not like · anything I had expected; they were unlike the Americans in the camp; even their dialects were different. The Yanks were so tall. Tanned by the sun, they had turned peculiarly yellow from Atabrine, the antimalarial drug. And then those Nazi helmets. We had not known that the American battle helmet had been changed from the tin hats of World War I to the modern ones, fashioned more in the German style.

Many of the lads I knew were hostages in the Education Building. I thought of the friend to whom I had given my chocolate and wondered whether we should ever see each other again. Then hunger had its way with me, catching me up in cramps, while the bedbugs fed themselves and mosquitoes whined inside my tattered net. My father's faint snoring lulled me almost to sleep. A few hours passed. The twist in my guts grew unbearable.

Dawn was lifting the night away. Outside the Annex a lone star pierced the sky over the acacia trees; a rich odor of bacon and ham came from a bivouac nearby. The troops had camped and built fires. I wandered closer and watched them cooking on their mess kits. They did not have nasal voices but deep familiar ones. The men were Negro soldiers, segregated from the yellow Atabrined troops in the front grounds. They were Ma Sanders' people. Then they saw me and gathered round. "Skin and bones," they said as they felt my arms and legs and ran their hands over my cage of bones.

"What's your name? They call me 'Heaven,'" said one of the soldiers.

"You hungry?" asked another.

And they fed me, frying tinned ham and eggs over their fire. But warm food is too much for the starving. I was going to be as sick as hell and didn't want the soldiers to know. So I managed to get away and in a moment retched and gagged, vomiting worms, bile and a mouthful of food.

5.

Tanks and riflemen surrounded the Education Building. A fitful knot of women, wives and mothers of the hostages, had spent the night watching the windows, fearful of further firing. From the top-floor windows young boys were waving and cracking jokes. My last distinct memory of Sweeney is at one of those windows yelling, "Hey, Prising — get me out of here!"

The walls of the building were scored by shot. An American soldier had been killed; others were wounded. A Japanese guard was dead. One hostage had been shot in the thigh, and another, an old man, had died of fright when his bed took fire from the shooting. Negotiations were in deadlock.

The front grounds of Santo Tomás had become an American military camp. Steadily through the night, soldiers had pitched tents and dug trenches and foxholes; now, surrounded by bazookas, howitzers and machine guns, they were building fires, heating their rations and oiling their gun mountings. Meantime, more tanks and truckloads of soldiers were coming through the Main Gate.

The encampment smelt of sweat, fried food and machinery. All the soldiers were friendly, eager to show us their M-1 rifles and grenades, to give us their rations, which they were tired of by now. The strain of battle burned from their eyes and they longed for furloughs. Holding mugs of coffee in their hands, they took time out to talk to us, leaning against their tanks — quaintly called "Georgia Peach" or "San Antone." They were worried that their women in the States were taking up with other men. Of the sad songs those soldiers sang or whistled, all but the most telling have long since been forgotten: "I'm going to buy a paper doll that I can call my own, a doll that other fellas cannot steal."

Every hour or so, a force of soldiers left the camp to battle in the surrounding district. Japanese snipers were firing into the camp; two had been caught scrambling over the roof of the adjacent seminary, disguised in the white robes of friars. Only a few streets in the vicinity of Santo Tomás were in American hands: Malacañang Presidential Palace was taken at midnight, the Japanese had abandoned Bilibid prison, and American tanks were storming Far Eastern University just south of the camp.

The Main Gate of Santo Tomás, which had been battered down the night before, was being repaired under heavy guard. I was accustomed to soldiers at the gate. Yesterday's guards had been Japanese and today's were American, the chief difference being that today's guards were not the enemy. They could understand that I wanted to get outside the walls to have a look round. The GI's gave me a pass, advising me to return in ten minutes.

Filipinos waiting for friends, husbands and former employers rushed over to me; we hugged and wept foolishly. They begged me to go back to Santo Tomás. "All the streets are mined," they warned. I laughed, telling them I needed a bit of a walk.

Mud was everywhere: water mains had burst in the street. Buildings were burning; a block of homes close by had been razed to the ground. A group of Yanks with hand grenades was stealing into a house across the street. Explosion. Smoke. No one came out of the house. My spirits sagged like my knees. I was afraid. It was as if the sun had been suddenly covered, a blackout in daylight. What I expected was an experience of total freedom; I wanted to be one of the first prisoners to leave the camp, but now as I stood in the street I realized that I was still a prisoner of war. Rubble blocked my way; a stuttering machine gun punctuated my despair: I turned back.

Inside the camp again, I made my way through the wide stretch of tanks, mess fires and trenches. Russian Harry and some other young boys were hanging about the encampment, puffing at their first smokes. Abiko, they said, had been buried with his face in the mud.

That night the Americans reached an agreement with Commandant Hayashi in the Education Building. The Japanese would be permitted to keep their weapons and be escorted to their front lines. Very early the following morning, when I was scrounging for breakfast in the front grounds, I saw them pass by. Some forty or fifty Japanese were surrounded by a hundred Yanks. Commandant Hayashi stumped along at the head of the contingent with Mr. Stanley, the interpreter, to one side of him and an American officer to the other. A wounded Japanese soldier was being wheeled by his comrades in a cart. Small bands of men and women followed them through the encampment, jeering and hooting — the women loudest of all — until the Japanese plodded out of the camp and the gates clanged shut.

What actually happened to those Japanese when they were being escorted to their front lines? Shortly before they reached their destination in Sampóloc, half a mile from Santo Tomás, a gang of Filipinos came down the street. The official version, I believe, was that, upon seeing the Filipinos, the Japanese scattered for cover and had to be coaxed back by their officers. This seems unlikely. Since they were under such heavy American guard it is much more probable, as the prevailing rumor had it, that the Japanese were met by an angry mob of Filipinos armed with bolos, hatchets and knives, who took them from front and behind and cut them to death. But I have never seen this in print.

6.

With the siege of the Education Building over and the Japanese escorted from camp, the building was immediately evacuated and searched for a time bomb or some similar sort of lethal souvenir. None was found. Believing that the worst was over, everyone attempted to resume the exultant spirits of the night when the Yanks arrived. By midmorning hundreds of war prisoners began drifting to the front of the Main Building. Word had got round that the Stars and Stripes would be unfurled in solemn ceremony in Santo Tomás, the largest concentration camp of American civilians in history.

Press photographers and newsreel men were prepared for the event. Many prisoners put on the best clothes they had left; the men hid their arms in long-sleeved shirts and each woman wore her most respectable dress. Few wished to look like prisoners of war — that would have been an admission of defeat. A sudden hush. Then as the banner was draped from the balcony over the entrance way, emaciated arms rose in salutation. Everyone tried to sing "God Bless America," hundreds waving and smiling till they wept, while children, heedless of formal celebration, scampered through the crowds trying to get in front of the press and newsreel cameras.

A day or two later, General Douglas MacArthur made a sudden brief appearance at Santo Tomás. He was inevitably mobbed by old friends, the fatuous, the curious and many a grizzled die-hard. I, of course, would not miss the opportunity to observe the general at close range as he stood greeting friends, mindful that his eagle profile was turned towards the larger part of his audience. With a flick of the wrist he scribbled his name for bashful youngsters pushed forward by their fulsome parents. General MacArthur gave the impression of a man who disdained affectation: the Supreme Commander of the Pacific Theatre of War made no pretense at being anything less than he was.

Before the general's visit, Japanese shells had exploded in Santo Tomás. Upon his departure the heaviest strikes began. Intermittently, through the subsequent days and nights, the Japanese cannon kept up their attack, while the American guns, placed within the grounds of our civilian prison camp, blasted at the Japanese.

Santo Tomás became a principal target. The Main Building, with its ostentatious tower and cross, took the brunt of the blows. Yet it was not the only building to be hit; shells burst in the Gymnasium and the entire south end of the camp stood in danger. Death rose up to greet prisoners of war, Filipino laborers, refugees and American soldiers alike. Even in the Annex, partly shielded by the Main Building, a girl was killed.

As time spaced itself out, after the insidious whining of shells and their blasts, we would begin to relax, hoping that the Japanese guns had made their final strike. The hour-long pauses would be broken by another queer drone — each sound was different from the one before — and then explosion, death. People who had gallantly withstood thirty-seven months of imprisonment broke down and wept; some became hysterical, others sank into bewildered apathy. Victory and a swift end to battle were what we expected; instead, we were under direct attack.

Only the first night remains distinct from the other days and nights of cannon fire. The camp lay in complete blackout. No one in the Annex could sleep as the shells came whining and smashing through the night, striking at the Main Building. Room Zero was close to the room that received the worst hits and I knew that my mother, with the other women from her room, was sitting up the night in the corridor. At first, my father refused to let me go to the Main Building; by midnight, however, when the worst of the shelling seemed to have stopped, he agreed that I should bring Mother back to our safer Annex corridor.

Shrieks, sobbing, voices calling for help. Plaster and masonry rattled as they fell. Smoke filled their air. In the darkness men were pulling bodies out of the rubble. Stretcher bearers were taking the wounded away. The dead were left till morning. Flashing my light on starved, sleepless faces, I searched the clutter of women in the corridor before Mother's room. Caught in the beam of my torch, Mother sat on the floor, staring at nothing. A woman lay sprawled like a child over her lap. My mother stared ahead, not recognizing me. Someone lent me a hand and we managed to lay the woman aside. I forced my mother up. Still she did not recognize me; she did not hear my voice; her eyes, unseeing and white, gazed past my light. The thin shape of a man approached me, saying that my mother was only suffering from shock. Taking her frail, skeletal hand in mine, I led my mother, as if she were blind, out of the Main Building and into the Annex.

Everyone was awake. The sharp voices of children were asking questions. I found Russian Harry on the prowl, so I sent him to fetch my father. When they reached us, we took Mother to the corridor outside of our quarters and Father bathed her head from his water jug. Her eyes swivelled distractedly, but by now she seemed dimly aware that she was with us. And softly, like a child crooning itself to sleep, she moaned, "No, no — no more now. I don't want any, any more . . ."

Russian Harry brought some brandy that the Yanks had given his sister. It made Mother choke, cough; then she came round a bit and recognized my father: "Is that you, Fred?" she said.

Mother never seemed to remember that night. She came out of her state of shock the next morning, but it affected her deeply, taking away parts of her memory with it. If at one time she had deliberately forgotten much of her childhood, this last shock effaced the more recent years and emphasized a characteristic vagueness which increased in her old age, often to the point of eccentricity.

When the shelling was over, a small girl roamed through the camp singing. Her mother had been struck dead in front of her. Now this girl with clear brown eyes, her hair chopped short as an urchin boy's, dressed like a ragamuffin in her torn dungarees and striped T-shirt, wove in and out among prisoners and groups of soldiers singing, "How beautiful is the moon in the tropic night." Hers was a light, childish voice, but she kept perfect tune. Her father was missing, her mother dead. She sang not because she was mad; she sang to give herself the courage to live.

7.

The Battle for Manila waged for thirty days and nights. General MacArthur's plans for an elaborate Victory Parade were hastily cancelled and he was obliged to take a brisk tour of the fighting in a jeep. More than three-quarters of the city would be laid waste by the Japanese and United States armies. Not until Manila became the most devastated city in Asia would the battle end.

After the Americans had captured Santo Tomás and the northern quarter of the city, the Japanese stiffened their resistance. While hundreds of thousands of civilians were trapped between the two armies, Manila was crushed by the frenzied Japanese and the methodical assault of American artillery. The massacre which we had feared for so long took place not in Santo Tomás but in the streets of Manila.

Before the American troops had reached the city, the Japanese had no definite plan of defense; in fact, part of the Imperial Army had taken to the hills. Upon the American invasion, the Imperial Navy launched a massive bombardment from their ships in the Pasig River. As the Americans closed in hard on the city, the remainder of the Imperial Army took a suicide stand. Placing their cannons in the belfries of churches or on hospital roofs, they shelled each section of the city they had lost. Gangs of Japanese fought from house to house, and in the face of certain death avenged themselves by killing any living being in sight. When crowds of Filipinos rushed to the churches for safety, they were butchered. Building after building was blasted by American artillery routing handfuls of Japanese. Manila exploded street by street. The city roared and crackled in flames and the fire spread with the wind. At night one could see the fiery timbers, as big as aeroplanes, riding the air. Still the Americans with their superior weaponry advanced, while the Japanese, their ammunition exhausted, tore through exploding streets, sabres and bayonets unsheathed, slaughtering the mobs of fleeing Filipinos. American tanks, flame throwers, bazookas and howitzers pushed on until another district of corpses and rubble was left in their wake.

The armless, the legless, the blood-spattered, an endless river of Filipinos flooded towards Santo Tomás, one of the few places of refuge — the prison camp where we white prisoners of war had been saved at the expense of a whole city of Orientals. In years to come, statistics could (give or spare a corpse here or there) number the Japanese and American battle deaths, but not the unknown, unnamed Filipino civilians who were massacred between those two armies.

In Santo Tomás, beside the commandant's bunker, a Red Cross dressing station was set up. The nurses and orderlies stationed here could give little more than first aid to the wounded refugees who streamed through the gates. Bandages, gentian violet and Vaseline were their only antidotes to the Battle of Manila. And since I was always hanging about, they soon set me to work rolling bandages and daubing minor wounds.

At noon, when the Main Gate closed, only one medic remained on duty at the dressing station where I was finishing up some bandages. A Filipino had somehow managed to get past the guards at the gate and was wheeling a makeshift wooden barrow up to us. Humped in the barrow lay the blood-soaked body of a woman, her black hair thickly crusted with dirt and dried blood. She was dead. In a sweat of anguish, the Filipino kept wringing his hands; he begged on his knees; he shrieked and stammered at the medic in broken English: "No, you go make her good. Make her alive. Please! Americans can do anything. Kill all Japs; win war. You can make her live, yes?"

The woman's face had been blown off. While the man continued to rave, we washed his wounds and dressed them. Then the medic had to send him away. It was helpless agony to have to watch the man wheel the barrow back towards the Main Gate, to have to hear him whimpering crazily at every jolt, not knowing what he could do with his precious bundle of flesh that had once been a living woman with a face.

The blood bath in Manila did not stop. While the slums of Tondo burnt to the ground, the business districts of Santa Cruz and Binondo blazed and smoked. Retreating south of the Pasig River, the Japanese blew up the bridges and then held out from the battlements of the Walled City. And as the Americans grimly advanced, fires and explosions burst out in Paco, Ermita, Malaté — in every quarter of Manila from which I used to hear the church bells ring.

Just as soon as our camp was fairly safe from shelling, the Americans projected films to thousands of spectators. War prisoners, refugees and soldiers sat on the ground before the Main Building and beyond the movie screen we could see the searing sheets of flame and the flash of cannon fire. For our entertainment there were Hollywood films, newsreels of jungle battles, Grable, Gable and Donald Duck.

Manila is burning. There, on the screen, is Al Jolson in blackface, his white gloves flickering as he clasps his hands, shuffles and sings. Behind me a boy is laughing as Jolson kneels and pleads, "Mammy, don't you know me? I'm your little baby." I turn round and see a Filipino lad with a gaunt, laughing face, his great black eyes as bright as life. We make friends, hugging each other while Jolson sings, "I'd walk a million miles for one of your smiles." And as I kissed him, I saw, under the army blanket thrown carelessly over his lap, the bandaged stumps of his knees.

His laughter is the only full, free laughter I have ever heard.

Most of the American troops in Manila visited Santo Tomás and I made scores of friends among them. I used to take those

Yanks up to the high observation tower of the Main Building. And they would stand solemnly, gazing through their binoculars at the panorama of annihilation that stretched far to the south and westerly out in the bay. Manila's harbor was choked with warships that had capsized or sunk — prows jutting out like coffins after an earthquake, the masts askew, like crosses that mark the dead.

Of all the men I took up the observation tower, Stan is the one I most clearly remember. Yet I saw him only four or five times. He was a gentle, twenty-two-year-old from Illinois, with a far-sighted stare. I had never heard anyone talk as Stan did. To him this war was part of the never-ending chaos of human misery, mankind's untold, unmeasured suffering that would persist through the ages while each civilization rose and fell. All personal grief and experience would be lost in that enduring chaos. And to the generations that replaced our own, it would be as though we had never lived.

In his pocket, Stan carried a dog-eared copy of the poetry of Hart Crane. He never read the poems aloud but would thrust the book at me or one of his buddies, pointing out a particular line or stanza. The men loved Stan; he was the dreamer, the scholar of their outfit. The last time I saw him, he gave me my first pint of beer, warning me in his half-melancholy, half-quizzical way not to get drunk.

Some days later, I met his comrades without him. They were embarrassed, unable to look me in the eye. It was Forlino who broke the news, Forlino the prankster gone clumsily earnest.

"We used to tell him 'Clear away the mist so you can see the mist.' Remember? Well, he walked into a booby trap . . . And I guess you know what *that* means."

Stan's dog tags and his copy of Hart Crane were sent back to his people in Illinois. I do not know where he is buried or even remember his full name.

8.

In the patio under the white heat of the ruthless sun, cheap, plywood coffins had piled up, filled with the rotting dead. No burial squad could work so quickly as that sun. In the smothering stench, nauseous after a lunch of greasy stew, I felt my heart beat up, my arms and legs twitch with life, with that absurd pride of simply being alive. Stifled by heat and the stink of corpses, I passed into the courtyard of squalid shacks, between those leaking, whitewashed boxes of the dead, and walked barefoot over the earth that swallowed up their blood.

The whole tide of my soul was rising and heaving within me. I had wandered into our cook shack where, scarcely a fortnight before, we had burnt books for fuel and boiled roots and weeds. Only one book was left, a dirty blue book. And when I fetched it down, it opened in my hands. A face in a photograph was gazing up at me. Dark brows. White hair. An old woman's face, vulnerable, expectant, full of life. Eleonora Duse, the tragic actress unique in a profession of artifice. It is the face of one who can still believe in the ridiculous miracle of individual suffering.

I kept looking into the face of Eleonora Duse. Then the knowledge gathering within me broke suddenly free, taking me farther than I had ever been; I knew that life still is holy. On the page beside the photograph, the words of Duse confirmed the mystery in her eloquent face: *Force et Confiance de Vivre* — Strength and Confidence in Life.

Seized by the discovery of this knowledge and all alive with it, I gripped the dirt with my bare feet until I grew into the immense energy of the sun. "And when these things begin to come to pass, then look up and raise your heads."

9.

On March 4, 1945, the United States Army declared the devastated city secure. The people began to emerge like rats out of the ruins. Ragged, starving, homeless, our friends flocked to the Main Gate to tell us they were alive, to beg for food and to bring word of those who had been killed in the carnage.

Before long we learned that Rosario had died in a massacre at the Malaté church. Old Doña Concepción Aguilar had survived her young niece and now lived in the kitchen of their house, the only room that victory had spared. Father Hinehan, Father Kelly and Father Lawlor had been arrested by the Japanese and taken with twenty other men to a house in Calle Cortabitarté. The Irish priests must have been executed. No witness to their deaths remained, nor were their bodies found.

In red Cuban heels, wearing bangles and beads that might once have been Woolworth's best, Terray's sister came to the camp. After she told Mother and me how Terray and the baby were crushed in the cellar, she went on to tell us how she herself had lived since.

"Then I got no house, no money and everything cost many pesos. I think maybe nobody is good no more. Americans make bombs and kill Terray, so I find some Jap and he go ask me to live in his house. Oh, mum, Japs is all bad — they want to fuck with the Filipina women."

Mother gave her a frosty glance but let the girl continue.

"When Americans make bombs on Manila every day, I know they going to come back soon. My old boy friend, he comes and tells to me that he fights for the guerrillas. So I let that Jap go sleep, then I steal his gun and give to my boy friend."

The Assumption Convent, which gave us sanctuary during the Japanese invasion, was requisitioned by the Imperial Army.

Mother Philomene Marie and seven of her sisters had remained in Manila, where they lived in a wing of the Don Vicente Madrigal's house, in the district of Paco. Here they were trapped during the battle for Manila.

The nuns were at mass on the morning of February ninth when a terrific explosion rocked the house. Rising from her prayers, Mother Philomene hastened to look after an elderly nun who was confined to her bed upstairs. Just as she reached the stairway came a second blast. By the time the other nuns found her, Mother Philomene lay caught in fallen furniture. Both her legs were shattered with shrapnel.

For the next two days, the nuns and more than thirty other civilians at Don Vicente's were in the direct line of fire. At every pause in the shooting, two young nuns would lug Mother Philomene to whatever air-raid shelter or dugout seemed safest. Wracked by pain and close to delirium, Mother Philomene kept worrying about her sisters, begging them to rest.

Towards evening of the third day there was a lull in the battle and once again the nuns removed Mother Philomene, this time to a cow shed — the one roof left by the flames. There was a shot; then the sharp retorts of crossfire. The young nuns wanted to take Mother Philomene back to the air-raid shelter.

"No, no — I'd take up too much room with these legs outstretched."

The nuns hesitated; the shots came faster now, and closer.

"Quick, sisters, run! Run to the shelter. Forget about me!"

And so Mother Philomene remained in the cow shed. By now she had spent three days in agony, being shifted to and fro, her legs swollen, shrapnel embedded to the bone. A man stood beside her, brewing coffee over a charcoal stove. The bullet aimed at the man took Mother Philomene instead. She was instantly killed.

Before that night had passed, all the other civilians were saved.

Whenever I think of Mother Philomene Marie, I remember the rustle of her wine-dark robes as she came striding towards me just before Manila fell to the Japanese. "Now you are in God's hands," she had said, forming an invisible shield around me, which served as protection not so much from danger as from fear. "Ten years old?" she had said on our last visit. "You are two numbers now. Quite grown-up — you will never be more than two." And I still can feel the force of her faith, a faith stronger than any creed.

The slim, gentle Alfredo, with his one golden tooth, was lost in the war. He vanished somewhere into the hills of Illocos Norte, his home province. Neither his cousins nor anyone who had known him as an orphaned boy ever saw him again.

In 1953, when Father and Mother were crossing the street in a Manila still rebuilding, a smart Rolls-Royce drew up to the curb, loudly sounding its horn. Looming was waving out of the chauffeur's window. His familiar, independent grin spread over his face and he still wore a flower at his ear. Yes, Looming would have got through the war. Somewhere in modern Manila he is alive today.

10.

In March of 1945 when I saw the ravages of Manila I had not yet learned my final lesson of the war. I knew only that life was holy and that I despised what had happened to my childhood city. It would be years before I discovered that contradictory rule of life which is so difficult to follow: One must not only remember, one must also forget. In those days I was concerned with what I must remember.

From north-west to south, straight as the carrion crow could fly, the bomb-cratered streets gaped and the mountains of wreckage ranged wide and far. Manila was still an occupied city. American jeeps, tanks and armored cars blundered through mud, through heaps of crashed brick and debris. In the avenues, bulldozers were at work heaving the rubble aside, clearing a way to let the conquerors pass. Some of the larger buildings remained, but they had burnt out and were crumbling within, their concrete facings so scored by shot and shell that tangles of iron framework were exposed like the veins of a butchered animal.

I rode through the desolation in a jeep. Flame trees had been stripped of their leaves as after a typhoon; palms stood erect with their heads lopped off. As we jerked past collapsing buildings, the corpse-stench rose in the tropic heat. Everywhere, destitute, half-naked people stooped like rag pickers. Manila had become a no man's land of cripples crutching about on laths salvaged from tottering houses. A blinded man with a hideously disfigured face begged us for food. Stunted children raised fingers in V for Victory as we passed. The soldiers in our jeep bought post cards of prewar Manila from a woman with an amputated arm. Gouged with wounds, blistered by burns, everyone went scavenging in and out of the carcasses of houses for anything they could eat or sell or save.

We lurched down towards the Escolta to find my father's office but were stopped by roadblocks. The entire business district had been razed. So we swivelled round, heading for an army pontoon bridge that spanned the Pasig River. Beside it, half submerged in water, lay the old Santa Cruz Bridge with burnt remnants floating by it and out to sea. To the right, like a mausoleum, stood the huge, hollow shell of the post office, where Stan had stumbled into a booby trap. Beyond, we could see the blasted remains of Jones Bridge which, despite its name, had been as graceful as any bridge in Paris.

Across the river, surrounded by monstrously broken, gutted walls was Intramuros, the Spanish city of Manila built in 1571. The seven gates that led into the citadel had toppled to ruins; the bombed-out churches and belfries hovered like skeletons over crushed stones. Few of its inhabitants had lived through the siege; the Walled City had served as a fortress in the Japanese suicide stand. The medieval arches and courtyards, the rococo church of Our Lady of Lourdes, were smashed to rubble by American artillery; mounds of ashes and burnt corpses sprawled over cobbled streets and winding narrow lanes. Three centuries of architecture had been turned into a vast oven.

Back again over the river, the jeep swung towards Quiapo and the Plaza Miranda where the baroque Quiapo Church stood whole, spared by fire and mortar: a serene monument survived. Inside the church a choir of crying babies mingled with the voices of women — refugees who had sought sanctuary in this church noted for its miraculous, life-sized black Nazarene. The homeless had camped themselves in the pews and along the aisles beneath the stations of the cross. It was mid-Lent by now and the statues and paintings were draped in violet and black. At a confessional near the massive carved-wood altar a stream of penitents waited, as if they had sins to tell.

The GI's with me were silent, awed by the survival of the Quiapo Church and by the shelter of mercy it bestowed upon the destitute. Oblivious of the crowd of refugees, a crippled hag in black rags crawled the length of the church on her knees, her black beads in her claws, groaning the Gloria: "As it was in the beginning, is now and ever shall be, world without end. Amen."

Out in the sun we wandered about in a reckless humor through the dead streets of Quiapo, clambering over hill-heaps of demolished houses, laughing, rolling the wheel of a carromata, taking turns kicking a big, rusted can. Suddenly someone shouted. A Yank had kicked the can into the severed arm and outstretched hand of a child that lay rotting in a ditch.

We came upon a garden where a whole tree stood, burnt to charcoal. There was a heavy stench. Over the rubbled yard a pariah dog limped guiltily away. Face upwards, beside a litter of scorched beams and stones, lay a dead Japanese soldier, putrid in the Manila sun. Flies swarmed the corpse, an enemy corpse which no one would bury. The eye sockets were alive, wriggling with maggots, and the mouth of the corpse, rigidly open, exposed a row of perfect teeth.

11.

There was dancing at Santo Tomás. The atmosphere was shot with hysterical sounds of survival, a maniacal impulse to celebrate, to forget, to have fun, any kind of fun, after the weeks of carnage. Most of the girls and younger widows found themselves soldier boy friends for the week, for the day, for the hour. Sex, which I had known about only theoretically, took place behind every bush and tree. In the mornings, when the little tots came out to play, they found the ground littered with condoms and blew them up like balloons.

Down several streets from the camp, whorehouses sprang from the rubble and queues of beery GI's stood wise-cracking before them, impatient for a three-minute fling.

Across from Santo Tomás, near a block of houses which had been spared, I watched a bevy of Filipina women crowding round a GI.

"Hey, you, Big Boy! You want to make pam-pam?"

The soldier bargained with a tin of corned beef, which he held over their heads like an auctioneer. He had his eye on the youngest girl — a shy thirteen-year-old who kept trying to hide behind the skirts of an older woman.

"I ain't gonna get me no syph or clap, no siree," said the soldier. "Prob'ly she's no virgin anyhow."

"Hell, I wouldn't screw one of them native women," muttered the Yank at my side.

My curiosity in the matter of sex was insatiable: I was always asking leading questions. The week after my twelfth birthday, I found a Marine lieutenant who taught me to masturbate in a sober lecture-demonstration behind the Japanese guardhouse.

It had been turned into a dance hall, hung with colored paper lanterns. A battered upright piano was stammering boogie-woogie to the squeals of forced laughter and the scuffle of dancing feet. The night air was strong with the smell of beer and whisky; light from the dance hall spilled out of the window and onto the lieutenant's lesson. Inside, the piano was going a-plink-plank to "Drum Boogie," while voices palpitated, "Beat me, Daddy, eight to the bar," faster, faster. And with a tug of the hand the Marine brought me to a jolt of pleasure and into adolescence.

By good fortune, the marine's lesson preceded a more clinical one. Into the shower room of the Main Building some soldiers brought a roaring drunk buddy, his bandaged penis oozing with blood and yellow pus. I had already heard a good deal about Signor Gonorrhea and the sight of the slobbering, venereal GI did not make me feel unduly squeamish. In fact, I was not so shocked as I had been in hospital when I saw a leper with his face eaten away. I had already been initiated into the mysteries of sex and, after the massacre of Manila, no merely curable disease could disgust me.

12.

Towards the end of March there were fewer battle-fraught GI's for me to take up the high observation tower, fewer army buddies to give me cigarettes and beer and take me for rides through the ruins in their jeeps. The lusty nights of booze and jitterbug were on the wane. Santo Tomás was invaded by brass, by the executives of the military machine. The hot-blooded soldiers who had fought the battles were replaced by a different breed — crew-cut robots with albino faces and ice water for blood.

By order of General MacArthur, a notice was posted informing us that we must accept offers of repatriation or leave camp:

the military wanted us out of Santo Tomás. The order was welcomed by many people — those who were passing through Manila at the outbreak of war or those who had been assigned to temporary posts by big business concerns. But for many who, like my father, had lost touch with their kin and native lands, it was an eviction.

Hundreds had already left for the United States or Australia. In April the major exodus would begin and Mother and I would sail for the United States. But there was no question of Father's leaving. He would stay with Filipino friends whose home in north Manila had been saved. Papa was sixty-six, though he looked well into his seventies. He would be judge of the races whenever they started again. Until that time he would try to salvage what he could of his tobacco business, though this proved a futile task since his ledgers, records and proof of money owing to him were burnt with his office. It would not be easy for him to begin again.

As for me, at the age of twelve, two periods of my life had closed; by this time I was well into my third. My early years had been a time of ease and plenty: like a child through his fingers, I had merely peeped at the world outside. This childhood had abruptly ended with the Japanese occupation of Manila when I was nearly nine years old. The fall of Manila forced me into boyhood, three years which even now seem the longest in my life. This was the time in which I learned to live through hope. The American invasion and the ensuing holocaust had shut my boyhood behind me. Within a month I saw my childhood city beaten flat, the people of Manila homeless, maimed or left for carrion. But I was not dead. I could look down at my arms, feet, legs; they were quick with life — I had awakened into youth. And where would my delirious youth lead me? We would soon be shipped to America and I wondered what the years ahead would bring. Would I bend myself to my environs, or could I make them bend to me?

My head was filled with adolescent fantasies; I was already
in revolt. The stage, I imagined, was where I belonged. Nor
could my mother check my extravagant dreams, which she
rightly considered ridiculous. She told me that she had no intention of becoming a backstage mother to a stilted boy. She
explained that the palmy days of the theatre, which I had read
about, had vanished with limelight and gaslight. Her own
decade on the stage, at the opening of the century, had been
the afterglow of that era of gaslight and grandeur. Since that
time, two world wars had intervened and the theatre had been
usurped by silent films, talkies and radio. Soon the public
would be sitting at home watching a box called television.

Of one thing, however, I was certain: I did not wish to go to
school or ever to be treated as a little boy again. The past three
years had provided an education far broader than any that was
available to me in this period of my precocious youth. I had
graduated, I would insist, from a venerable university which had
been founded by Spain in 1611. Was there a question of dip-
loma? I had taken a degree of experience from the Royal and
Pontifical University of Santo Tomás.

No drums, no music; the funeral was over. A convoy of army
trucks awaited us before the Main Building. Father's grey
eyes were dim, his face inscrutable as he kissed us goodbye, making me promise to take care of my mother. I climbed up into the
truck. In my little cardboard suitcase I had kept the photograph
of Eleonora Duse, some shards of shrapnel from our home by
the sea and those Christmas gifts of 1941 that had gone through
the war with me, my camera and dominoes. Mother sat beside
me in the truckful of prisoners of war. None of us had much to
say. We could scarcely lift our hands to wave.

It had been night when we first arrived at Santo Tomás and
we were singing, but now in this plain daylight there was no
need of song: we had kept our courage up. The massive

cenotaph of the Main Building, still scabbed from shellfire, stood heavily behind the acacia trees. We passed through the Main Gate and then plunged into the graveyard city of Manila. No one wept; no one spoke. With dry, scorching eyes I looked back in hatred at what we were leaving behind — at the war and the city of the dead.

For my life, for my experience, for the lessons of the war, I was thankful. If I had an enemy it was not the Japanese but war itself. And I knew that soldiers of both sides were the recruits of involuntary obedience, victims of ignorance and nationalism: the last vestige of slavery in modern times. Had it not been for the war I should not have known hunger, imprisonment; I might have grown to manhood in smugness without having shared the lot of millions in the world at war. Above all, I should never have recognized the holiness of human life. And I mourn not for myself but for the others, the losers: the legions of the maimed, the incurably insane and the dead.

All things fall and are built again. This rubble shall soon be overgrown by weeds, those weeds uprooted and the rubble replaced by a new city built by the living. To that new city I say: Manila, *Mabuhay,* may you live in peace and thrive; and to the old: Manila, Goodbye.